SOCCER CZARS

SOCCER
CZARS

A compelling insight into the lives
of the tycoons running the big clubs – and
British football

JASON TOMAS

MAINSTREAM
PUBLISHING

EDINBURGH AND LONDON

First published in 1996 by
MAINSTREAM PUBLISHING COMPANY
(EDINBURGH) LTD
7 Albany Street
Edinburgh EH1 3UG

ISBN 1 85158 774 8

A catalogue record of this book is available from the British Library

Typeset in Monotype Perpetua and Gill Sans
Printed and bound in Great Britain by Butler & Tanner Ltd

Contents

1. Money Money Money   7

2. Chairmen 1, Managers 0   39

3. Young Guns   71

4. The Thrill of the Chase   95

5. Deadly Doug and Blaster Bates   116

6. Fan Power   141

7. The Balancing Act   171

8. The Way Ahead?   183

ONE

Money Money Money

One of the highlights of the guided tour of Arsenal FC is entry into the imposing Highbury boardroom, an inner sanctum displaying all the traditional good taste you might expect of a club with their historic football image and history of success.

As you soak up the atmosphere, you imagine what it would have been like to be a fly on the expensive wood-panelled wall when the club, noted for setting the highest moral and ethical standards, were going through the embarrassment of the recent transfer market 'bungs' scandal involving their manager George Graham. Your eyes focus on the directors' chairs around the table in the centre of the room and you immediately notice that the seat at the top, reserved for the chairman, is bigger and plusher than the rest.

The other difference is that it has five legs.

The extra leg was added at the front, to give it more stability, some years ago. This, according to Arsenal historians, was because one incumbent rocked the chair back and forth during a board meeting to relieve his gout – and ended up in an undignified heap on the carpet.

Such are the changes that have taken place in the game, one suspects that if the gentleman was still around, he would need to have his chair bolted to the floor, and to have a seat-belt attached.

There are some things with which he would be familiar. As in the past, and as one would expect in an environment in which not all the clubs start on a level playing-field in terms of financial resources, there are still cases of chairmen putting their own club's interests before those of the game and allowing suspicion and envy to undermine their relationships.

He would recognise, too, the need for many of those in power in British football to have their egos massaged. It is said that inside every hard-headed, successful businessman – and especially the self-made tycoon who has clawed his way to the top from a humble start – is someone yearning for public love and acclaim. In that respect, professional football, through its popularity and the emotions it provokes, still provides as effective a platform as ever for chairmen to bring to life any fantasies of being worshipped as heroes.

Hence the other aspects of the game that have remained more or less the same: the tendency for clubs to chase the top players, at a price in transfer fees and salaries that seemingly only a small handful can comfortably afford, and for managers to be sacked, rather than the chairmen who appointed them, when things go wrong.

But in lots of other ways, the men who run Britain's leading clubs, and the way they operate, have changed beyond recognition.

The turning point came with the explosion created by the chairmen and club owners in 1992, when the 22 clubs which made up the First Division of the Football League, faced with massive costs in developing their stadiums to comply with the all-seater demands of the Taylor report, broke away to form an élite self-contained league of their own – the Premiership – under the auspices of the Football Association.

The breakaway had its roots in two documents, from the Football League and FA, giving recommendations on how English football could catch up on the progress of the game in other countries. The FA's 'Blueprint for the Future' spotlighted the need for English football to concentrate on quality rather than quantity; to reduce the ridiculously high number of matches played (or rather matches of little importance or national interest) so that the game could be presented as a more marketable package and the England team could be given the opportunity to punch their full weight.

The breakaway also had its roots in the desire of the big clubs to escape a structure which they had long insisted had stunted their growth. The formation of the Premiership meant that, instead of having to share the income from television and sponsorship with the 70 clubs below them in the four-division Football League, the big clubs could keep all the money to themselves. Without so many mouths to feed, in terms of their responsibilities towards the Football League as a whole, the top-division clubs, who attracted most of the attention anyway, would be able to take charge of their own destiny. They could move forward more smoothly and quickly.

Many critics believe that the Premiership has become merely another name for a 20- or 22-headed monster, an argument based on the premise that the FA has much less control over those clubs than the Football League had. Moreover, with each Premiership club having one vote, the biggest clubs – now forming a distinct league within a league – again face the problem of being shackled.

What nobody can deny, however, is that the Premiership is a monster with a gargantuan appetite for money. You only have to look at what the Premiership clubs receive from TV (albeit at an apparent cost of having sold their souls to this medium through the high number of matches screened live) to appreciate this point. When the Premiership started, it did so with the boost of a five-year BSkyB–BBC agreement potentially worth more than £300 million – a staggering sum, indeed, compared with the Football League's £44 million for the previous five-year deal with ITV and, before that, the £3 million a season from its joint ITV and BBC contract.

The TV figures became even more mind-boggling in June 1996, when the Premiership clubs agreed new four-year BSkyB–BBC deals which, from August 1997 to May 2001, will bring in £743 million. That increase, which will mean each club getting an average of around £8 million per season, is expected to become greater still for the leading clubs when pay-per-view TV comes into being in Britain.

The new contract with Sky provides for a review after two years, by which time it is anticipated that digital technology will have evolved sufficiently in the UK for every Premiership match to be screened live.

A report on the subject in *World Soccer* magazine in September 1996 emphasised the roads that are opening up for the likes of Manchester United and Newcastle when it stated: 'Pay-per-view is the key to even greater riches [from TV] and not one European country has yet begun to capitalise on this consumer-driven phenomenon. But Italy starts this season, France intends to, and England, Spain, Germany and Holland may do so next year. The advantages of pay-per-view from an operator's standpoint is control over the signal. Take the example of a Milan fan. The supporter, if he or she lives outside the Milan region, can subscribe to live coverage of all Milan's 34 home and away league matches at an overall cost of £215, the equivalent of £6 a match. A fan who lives within the Milan region can subscribe to all the club's 17 away league games at an overall cost of £129. Once the system is up and running, it is expected that a top match – such as a Milan or Turin derby – would be offered on a one-off basis at £13 to out-of-region fans, while a middle-of-the-table match would be offered on a one-off basis at £8.50.'

But the paragraph which will really have caused the eyes of Premiership chairmen to sparkle was the one that pointed out: 'European football has a long way to go before it drains television of the oceans of cash still waiting to pour into the accounts of the top clubs.'

All of which helps explain why clubs have been paying increasingly lavish sums on player transfer fees and wages – why, for example Newcastle bought Alan Shearer in the 1995–96 close season for a record £15 million, and Middlesbrough, who were on the brink of bankruptcy just a decade ago, added the Italian striker Fabrizio Ravanelli to their already costly list of foreign stars at a transfer fee of £7 million and reported salary of £42,000 a week.

Even Wimbledon, the poor relations of the Premiership who have turned pleading poverty into an art form, felt bold enough to break the £1 million transfer barrier for the first time, buying full-back Ben Thatcher from Millwall for £1.84 million.

There are other ways in which football's earning capacity since the formation of the showcase Premiership has been mirrored. In the second year of the Premiership, Carling bought the 'title' sponsorship of the competition for £12 million over four years, £500,000 more than Barclays paid for their *six-year* sponsorship of the old Football League. Then there is the money being spent at clubs by the fans – and not just in admission prices.

Football in England, helped in no small measure initially by the impact of the national team in the 1990 World Cup finals in Italy, has become fashionable again, with the result that millions have been added to the clubs' income figures relating to merchandising, sponsorships, ground advertising, executive boxes, function suites, publishing and stadium restaurants and bars.

Views are divided on whether all this has been good for the game. Many would argue that today's chairmen, with their flair and drive and astute development of their stadiums, have merely taken professional football into the 20th century after decades spent in a time warp. Others, though, prefer to sum up the whole situation in one word: greed.

They condemn the way the rich are continually reaching out for greater prizes, with no compunction about leaving the poor lagging further and further behind. One expert who pulls no punches on the subject is Alex Fynn, the former deputy chairman of Saatchi and Saatchi. As one of Britain's leading authorities in the field of sports marketing, Fynn, in addition to advising a number of top club chairmen throughout Europe, was given the job of investigating the commercial potential of English football in general and the Premier League in particular – on behalf of the FA – when the breakaway was at the planning stage. Fynn, the co-author of highly acclaimed books on the political side of football, takes a cynical view of where the chairmen and club owners have led the game: 'The fact is that most of these people, having achieved a degree of power and status, are a bit like medieval barons. The clubs are their fiefdoms – they decide what the rules are, and if they perceive that something is going to affect the success of their clubs, they are unlikely to feel bound to put up with it by a common code of honour or anything like that.

'They are no different to the people who run the big clubs on the Continent. The difference is that the system in England is geared to their [the big clubs'] own vested interests. It is not necessarily the clubs' fault. I would not go as far as to say that the chairmen engineered this situation, but they are certainly taking advantage of it. In other countries, the clubs outside the top division might be looked upon as second-class citizens, but it is considered very important – and rightly so – that they are kept in the same system. It is a question of the sum total of the whole being greater than its individual parts. In England, the only thing that matters is the Premiership, which I think is wrong.'

Since the formation of the Premiership, football at the top level has represented a gravy train. Never before have the rewards for staying on it been so lavish; and never before has the price paid for falling off it been so calamitous.

Deloitte and Touche spelt it out loud and clear in their report on the balance-sheets of clubs for the 1994–95 season. It showed that nearly 70 per cent of the total income of the Premiership and Football League clubs – £468 million – was brought in by those in the Premiership; and that while the Premiership clubs made an over-all profit before transfer fees of £49 million, their Football League cousins made a loss of £22.5 million.

It says much about the importance of being aboard that gravy train – the ultimate destination of which is almost certainly a European Super League – that influential club owners in the Premiership like Blackburn's Jack Walker, Newcastle's Sir John Hall, Everton's Peter Johnson and Tottenham's Alan Sugar have pumped many millions into their clubs between them. It is also highlighted in the ticket-hall of the First Division, where the combined club backing of Wolves' Sir Jack Hayward, Birmingham's David Sullivan and Derby's Lionel Pickering is similarly lavish.

In Scotland, too, the advantages of big money and big ambitions in driving a club forward have been seen by the David Murray-inspired revitalisation of Rangers, a club who have dominated the championship to the extent that the trophy now appears their own personal property. Notwithstanding the massive debt he inherited, Murray picked up one of the biggest soccer bargains of all time when he bought the club for just £6 million in the mid-1980s, when the previous owner, the American-based Lawrence Marlborough, ran into financial difficulties with his construction company. Rangers had been one of British football's so-called sleeping giants before Marlborough and his team manager Graeme Souness got to grips with it. With Murray in control, in tandem with Souness, who also owned a big slice of the club's shares by then, controlling Rangers became more and more like having a licence to print money. The Glasgow club have developed as a business to such an extent that they have almost outgrown the environment in which they are based. The same situation – that of starting to squeeze the lemon dry financially in your own country – is starting to concern their English counterparts.

That professional football in Britain has been transformed from a sport into a multi-million-pound business is endorsed by the 'Footie Index', a Scottish company 'designed to give a representative financial picture of the UK football sector'. In September 1996, it reported: 'The top ten clubs in financial terms are now worth more than £1 billion. Gross in the value of the clubs has topped 300 per cent in only 12 months, making it one of the fastest-growing sectors in British business.'

To traditionalists, it is an industry in which those at the helm – mega-powerful entrepreneurs – could even be said to be using football as a backdrop to a compelling game of their own, a game where the head is put before the heart; where professional football is taken away from its emotional, idealistic working-class roots in favour of maximising its financial potential; where rich men strive to score points off each other through the income they can generate.

It is a power game in which, metaphorically, blood is liable to be spilled all over the boardroom carpets. What, you wonder, would that port-sipping Arsenal chairman, who characterised the sober, stiff-upper-lip Establishment hierarchy for which the club were renowned, make of the much-publicised bitter feuds between Alan Sugar and Terry Venables, or between Chelsea's Ken Bates and Matthew Harding? Or of the fact that some chairmen, far from shunning the media spotlight, sometimes appear to relish basking in it?

They get plenty of opportunities to do so, as the upmarket soccer magazine *FourFourTwo* pointed out when observing that the only chairmen of the 1970s that one could readily name were Leeds United's Manny Cussins, Burnley's Bob Lord and Manchester United's Louis Edwards, and that 'these days, players can't get media coverage because the hack pack are too busy interviewing their chairmen'.

The former Tottenham chairman Irving Scholar, who shares with Bates the distinction of having written a book about his experiences on the board, would seem the last person to decry this. Nonetheless, Scholar, insisting that his tome was meant as an exercise in putting the record straight on his much-criticised stewardship of Spurs (as opposed to a glorification of himself) says: 'Few people would know of many of the club chairmen and owners but for their links with football. Previously, the only publicity they got was when they announced their businesses' half-year and full-year results, and that was it. But they go into football, and they are dominating the back pages. They might only have been to a handful of games in their lives, but suddenly they're experts and everybody wants to listen to them. That's when ego takes over. Ego should play no part in the game in my opinion, but it does.'

Scholar himself, whatever his faults, was noted for his genuine love of Tottenham and for his deep knowledge of the club and the game. Manchester United manager Alex Ferguson, recalling the period when he was boss at Aberdeen and became involved in negotiations with Scholar to take over as manager at Tottenham, took delight in trying to get the better of the Spurs man on football quiz questions. He rarely did. So Scholar could rightly claim to be more in tune with the game than most but, as he says, 'When I was involved with Tottenham you never heard me shout my mouth off here, there and everywhere. I find it difficult to admire chairmen who do. You know the ones I mean; with them, it's just a question of turning on the lights, giving them a microphone and asking what song they would like to sing. What do they think about this, what do they think about that? It's rent-a-quote.'

Whatever the merits of the argument that today's club figureheads have become too dominant for the game's good, there can be no doubt that the atmosphere emanating from club boardrooms is nothing like what it was at Ipswich in the days when the club was under the delightfully eccentric Old Etonian command of John Cobbold (chairman, 1957–76) and his brother Patrick (chairman, 1976–91). Even then, Ipswich were a club apart, as was emphasised when, during a period in which the club were in relegation trouble, John proclaimed: 'There is no crisis here. The only time there is a crisis is when we run out of white wine in the boardroom.'

The Cobbolds, nephews of former Prime Minister Harold Macmillan and grandsons of the ninth Duke of Devonshire, maintained a family boardroom dynasty that had begun when their father – influenced by the example of his fellow Old Etonians, the Hill-Woods, at Arsenal – brought professionalism to the club in 1936.

To both men, football was 'fun'. Thus, when he first met Norwich chairman Robert Chase, Patrick (or Mr Patrick, as he was commonly known) found it impossible to resist the temptation to compliment him on the expensive camel coat he was wearing as he helped him take it off – only to hurl it into the far corner of the room instead of hanging it up. It was that sense of 'fun' that made him subject any visiting chairmen he did not like to the sort of pre-match boardroom meal that even the most basic works canteens could have bettered. 'One chairman – I won't mention his name – actually liked it,' Cobbold recalled, laughing.

That chairman was Manchester City's Peter Swales. Chase, through his hard-headed business approach to the game, was also targeted by Cobbold in this way. 'Before one match there on Boxing Day, the Norwich directors and I were told that there was a buffet laid on for us in the boardroom,' Chase recalls. 'There was no food in the room, but suddenly a man wearing white gloves came in, holding this lovely tray above his head. When he lowered it, there were just six cold legs of chicken on it. That's all we had. That's how peculiar he was. But I think he was a very fair, warm and genuine man.'

The Cobbolds, whose millions were made in the brewery business that once bore their name, were indeed 'old money' gentlemen to a fault. The players looked upon them as kindly uncles. Their managers – who included Sir Alf Ramsey and Bobby Robson – found them the most liberal of men to work for. Such was the Cobbolds' respect for the professional expertise of their managers that they were reticent even about enquiring what their team would be.

Sometimes the chairmen directed their sense of humour at themselves. Patrick was fond of recalling that during a strike at the brewery, the pickets, on catching sight of him and his brother approaching the gates would shout: 'Oh, it's Mr John and Mr Patrick – they can go in, they don't do anything anyway.' They had the same rapport with their football club employees. Bobby Robson recalls that when Patrick fell asleep in the team coach *en route* to an away match – as he was liable to do after his customary lunchtime wine – the manager took the chicken out of his sandwiches. Some time later, on a pre-season trip to Spain, Robson started tucking into a large lobster only to find that all the meat had been removed from it and replaced with bread and mayonnaise. 'That will teach you to steal my chicken,' Mr Patrick had remarked.

So, the mere mention of the word 'Ipswich' was to conjure visions of everybody – fans included – with smiling faces.

Not all chairmen were like that – far from it. One notable exception was Burnley's Bob Lord, regarded as the most outspoken and confrontational of the chairmen breed during his authoritarian reign at Turf Moor. Others who readily spring to mind as having stood out from the rest include Elton John (whose partnership with Graham Taylor propelled Watford up the yellow brick road from the old Fourth Division to the First in ten years) and the larger-than-life tyrannical figure of Robert Maxwell at Oxford United.

The majority of chairmen in the old 92-club Football League, dismissed as a legion of 'butchers, bakers and candlestick-makers', were generally seen but not heard, at least publicly. Their business interests rarely stretched beyond the towns and cities in which their clubs were situated. They looked upon their involvement in the game, which often stemmed from inheriting family shares in their local clubs, as little more than a prestigious hobby through which the desire to contribute to their communities could be combined with impressing their friends and gaining some measure of public recognition.

But whatever nous they had shown in building up their own businesses, most seemed to leave it at the front entrance when they went into their football clubs. They would argue that they were prevented from taking their soccer roles more seriously even if they had wanted to do so because of the old Football League rule barring any director from being paid for his services. A much more pertinent factor was that a club's potential income from non-football activities was only a fraction of what it is nowadays.

So, to a great extent, chairmen were happy to let their managers and club secretaries run the show and bask in the reflected glory of a good performance on the field each Saturday. To the public, they were stereotyped as a group of privileged old fuddy-duddies with watch chains. To the professionals, it was perhaps typical of the way that chairmen and their boardroom colleagues were perceived that the autobiography of the former Sunderland and England star Len Shackleton included a blank page entitled 'What the average club director knows about football'.

Like Tommy Docherty, whose success as an after-dinner speaker has been founded on jokes at the expense of numerous chairmen who hired and fired him during his managerial career, Brian Clough was every bit as entertaining on the subject of boardroom figure-heads as Shackleton was. But towards the end of his career, even Clough was moved to agree that the managers and players employed by them to get good results on the field had become embroiled in a totally different ball game. 'Hooligans in football?' he remarked. 'Well, there's the 92 Football League chairmen for a start.'

It was not a jibe that one would make in the company of Alan Sugar, the notoriously belligerent and abrasive Amstrad electronics supremo, or the other formidable figures holding the purse strings at the Premiership clubs: Blackburn's Walker and Everton's Johnson, whose personal fortunes have been estimated at more than £300 million and £100 million respectively; Newcastle's Hall, a comparative pauper (his personal fortune is reckoned to stand at £37 million) but arguably the most dynamic member of the current group; Ken 'Blaster' Bates, whose outspoken comments make him the closest modern-day equivalent to Bob Lord; and Aston Villa's 'Deadly' Doug Ellis, who has a lengthy list of managerial sackings to his name.

Clough's comment does have some relevance with regards to the manner in which these men have provoked a change in the game's traditional values and ideals. For one thing, not all chairmen nowadays can claim to have had a lifelong affinity with their clubs. Bates had spells in the boardrooms of Oldham and Wigan before joining Chelsea and rescuing them from bankruptcy; Johnson was a Liverpool season-ticket-holder for more than 20 years, and then chairman of Tranmere Rovers, before forking out £10 million to buy control of Everton through underwriting a new shares issue. Such cases suggest that a number of chairmen nowadays are businessmen first and football fans second; that their attitude is similar to that of players and managers who move to bigger clubs to further their careers.

The sight of the urbane, usually diffident Johnson getting carried away by the excitement of watching his team play – a 'white-knuckle job' is how he describes it – underlines the point. For example, Johnson, recalling Everton's 1–0 win over Manchester United in the 1995 FA Cup final, says, 'At the final whistle, I jumped to my feet and threw my arms in the air, and suddenly realised this might not have been the right thing to do with the Duchess of Kent beside me in the Royal Box. But I just thought: "Sod it – we've just won the Cup," so I did it again.'

The Wirral-born Johnson, whose core business, the Park Foods hamper company, had an annual turnover of some £140 million, was no less enthusiastic and animated about Liverpool when he followed them, and about Tranmere. He spent seven years as Rovers' chairman, joining them (and at the same time putting up a rescue package to save them from collapse) in 1987. To him, the £100,000 it cost to buy the 18 per cent shareholding of their departing chairman, the American lawyer Bruce Osterman, was 'beer money', although he adds that it was only the starting point of his financial backing there: 'I prefer not to tell you what it [the final bill] came to.' Until then, he stresses, it had never been his intention to get involved in the running of a football club. 'When one of the Tranmere directors approached me to ask if I could save the club, I initially said: "No, I can't really – I follow Liverpool and I've got my work to do." But the challenge did seem interesting and it did whet my appetite. About three weeks later, I mentioned it to a pal – Frank Court – after we'd been out for a drink. "Oh, Peter, come on – let's do it," he said. So we went along to a Tranmere match, and I said: "I'll come and save you, but I am not going to come to the matches." This didn't bother them. "We don't mind," they said. But it doesn't work like that. Within six weeks, the white-knuckle job for me was not at Liverpool; it was at Tranmere.'

With Frank Court, a builder, installed as vice-chairman and chief executive to oversee the day-to-day running of the club (he subsequently took over as Tranmere chairman), Johnson 'had a lot of fun'. Under his command, Tranmere improved their stadium and their team, gaining promotion to the Third Division in 1989 and to the Second in 1991.

But Johnson admits that, having been hit by the football chairman bug, he became frustrated by Tranmere's inevitable inability to escape the Merseyside shadow of Liverpool and Everton. During an interview in the summer of 1995, he told me: 'Tranmere were never going anywhere before Frank and I arrived. The joke was that, before we got there, people thought the name was "Tranmere Rovers Nil". We changed that, but we couldn't break the mould of the big clubs getting the biggest crowds. You just can't get away from it.

'The potential at Tranmere was limited. In fact, if you look at the figures, the financial position there is now worse than it was when I was involved in the club – it has to be, because of the growing gap between their income and the money they have to spend to keep improving.

'In the early days, with a benefactor like me behind the club, it didn't matter. Things could go forward. With a benefactor like Osterman, who lived in San Francisco and wasn't putting any money in, that was it. They were getting 1,800 people in when I got there and the break-even figure would be 2,500. Now, to get it up to 2,500, you would have to spend more money on players, so that the break-even figure would become 4,000, and so it goes on. I remember the day we clinched promotion from the Fourth Division – a beautiful sunny May day when more than 15,000 turned up to see us play Crewe. You know, I don't think we ever had such a big gate again, despite the fact that we went on to get into the Second Division and make a strong challenge to get into the Premiership. Now, if we could have had 15,000 or 16,000 in there every time, I may well have stayed. But I must say I am glad I didn't.'

No doubt he is also glad to be in a position where the Tranmere public can't accuse him of having made a profit from his links with the club. 'There was no profit to be made. We had to borrow, and that does impact on the share valuation.'

Johnson does not go as far as to say that his departure to Everton has been a massive blow to Tranmere. Nonetheless, on the subject of clubs finding figureheads to lift them, it is easy to sympathise with Tranmere, and clubs like them, when he says: 'You've got to find someone rich enough to do it, who is a football fan, and there are not that many about. People would get a lot of enjoyment out of Tranmere but, let's face it, if you are that wealthy, you want one of the top ten, don't you?'

Getting his hands on Everton was an ambition that took Johnson 18 months to fulfil. It was a tortuous process, mainly because of the opposition to his bid for the club – by Lady Granchester, the daughter of the previous owner, the late John Moores – on the grounds that he wasn't a 'blue'. According to Johnson, it all boiled down to a misinterpretation of Sir John's will. 'She said that her father had stipulated that the shares had to go into "safe blue hands", but John Moores Jnr [one of the two sons who inherited the shares] maintained that the actual wording said that they had to go into "a safe pair of hands".'

To look at Johnson's success as a businessman, and the somewhat conservative Establishment hierarchy of the Moores family, is to invite the feeling that there could be only one winner. As Johnson says, 'I think I am quite shy – I don't seek the limelight – but I do have a certain amount of toughness which says that if I want something, I have to go and get it.'

The same could be said of Alan Sugar, the son of an east London Jewish rag-trade worker, whose tenacity has proved to be astonishing by any standards. He became Tottenham's unlikely knight in shining armour, in tandem with Terry Venables, in June 1991. Tottenham plc (under Scholar, they had become the first English club to become a public company) were reportedly £11 million in the red then, but Sugar hardly appeared brokenhearted over the club's situation. He had to fork out around £8 million to buy Scholar's 62 per cent controlling interest and, under public company law, he was also obliged to make the same offer to all the other shareholders. Nobody could have had any illusions about his mentality when he said, matter of factly: 'I have not invested in a football club. I have invested in a company that owns one.'

It will not have escaped those with cynical, suspicious minds that being a chairman of a popular football club is good for business. It gave Sugar and Amstrad a higher profile among the football-loving free-spending young men who represented the company's most lucrative market. Furthermore, there was a boost in the sales of the satellite dishes that Amstrad supplied for BSkyB television following the latter's success in beating ITV in the battle between the two companies to land the exclusive contract to televise Premiership matches live.

Uppermost in those cynical minds is the fact that BSkyB's over-lord, Rupert Murdoch, had always been a strong supporter of Sugar. The picture becomes even more intriguing when you wind the story forward to May 1992, when the 22 Premiership clubs met to discuss and vote on the BSkyB and ITV offers. By all accounts Sugar himself readily acknowledged he was in an embarrassing position; and Arsenal's vice-chairman, David Dein, drew even more attention to the Spurs supremo's vested interest in the matter when he called for a vote to stop Tottenham taking part. But the chairmen, clearly in an ultra-democratic mood, voted overwhelmingly against Dein's proposal.

Not surprisingly, Sugar gave a persuasive argument for accepting the BSkyB offer. He was also involved in the most bizarre incident of the affair. Early in the morning of that meeting at a London hotel – with BSkyB having been the first to reveal their hand in the bidding for this prized contract – ITV's Trevor East handed a letter outlining his company's offer to Rick Parry, the Premier League's chief executive, and all the club representatives. Later, while he was reading a newspaper in the hotel lobby, he overheard Sugar talking on the phone nearby. It soon became apparent to him that Sugar was revealing details of ITV's offer, and he concluded that Sugar was doing so to BSkyB. 'You don't seem to understand what I'm talking about,' Sugar was bellowing. 'These are the figures, take them down. You'd better get something done. You'd better get someone down here quickly. Blow them out of the water.' Sugar was not alone in being accused of tipping off BSkyB – so, too, was Parry, who admitted as much during the court case over ITV's claim that they had been fouled.

Notwithstanding the question of whether Parry marked BSkyB's card before Sugar did, the fact is that the satellite company increased their offer; and that Parry, having taken the details of it over the phone in another room, presented it – verbally – to the chairmen. They voted 14–6 in favour of accepting the BSkyB deal; when this was announced publicly, the news added £7 million to Amstrad's stock exchange valuation.

During the early part of his Tottenham reign, Sugar did little to disprove the view that some chairmen have no 'feel' for the game and, more specifically, for the cultures of their clubs. His justification for calling himself a Tottenham supporter stemmed from his having occasionally been taken to see them play by his father as a boy. But those who got into discussion with him about Tottenham's background, the traditions established by brilliant teams such as the one that achieved the Championship and FA Cup double in 1961, were left with the thought that the new chairman must have had a Spurs-magic bypass operation.

One popular story concerns Sugar's look of puzzlement when someone talked about the Tottenham double under Bill Nicholson. 'What double?' he was reputed to have said. Sugar's lack of knowledge of the game, and especially the soul of the game, was one aspect of the man that Terry Venables – inevitably much more popular than Sugar among the fans – tried to exploit during his bitter wrangle with the chairman over his sacking as Tottenham's chief executive. According to Venables, Sugar kept asking him why Tottenham could not adopt the same approach to the game as Wimbledon, a club whose need to sell their star players in order to survive has caused them to become masters at making transfer-market profits and bricks without straw through their somewhat pragmatic performances on the field. One report claimed that Sugar wanted to sign Russian players after the disintegration of the Soviet Union, repeatedly rationalising the idea on the grounds that they would be cheap.

'He can be hands-on in his other businesses because he knows them from top to bottom,' Venables once said. 'I don't think he knows football the same way. He just wants full control. He wants to play with his train set.'

Nowadays, Sugar is a considerably more credible football figure than he was. Many of the initial misgivings about him have faded or even been revealed as misconceptions. He has certainly become more football-oriented. Tony Berry, Tottenham's deputy chairman, has said: 'When he came into the game, the attraction factors were 80 per cent business and 20 per cent football. Now, it's getting to be the other way around.' Sugar, who according to one insider has learnt enough about the game to be looked upon by his Premiership colleagues as one of the chairmen who talks the most sense on political issues, is occasionally even seen watching the players in action at Tottenham's training ground.

It might well rankle with him, though, that he has yet to gain the same affection from the fans as Jack Walker has achieved at Blackburn. All the present Premiership club leaders have a problem on that score, because the 62-year-old Walker, following the sale in 1989 of his family steel business to British Steel for £330 million, has had no compunction about handing over £54 million of it – as a gift – to bring success to his beloved Blackburn. On top of this, the most recent Blackburn accounts, to the year ending 1995, reveal that he also contributed £17.1 million as an interest-free loan, all but £5 million of which carries no set repayment date.

Not surprisingly, the injection of so much dosh has had a dramatic effect on the fortunes of his home-town club. It has transformed Ewood Park stadium and, more pleasing to Rovers' long-suffering supporters, it has restored their team at the top after years in the doldrums. Under Walker's patronage, Blackburn, quite apart from tempting Kenny Dalglish to join the club as manager at a time when they were languishing in the old Second Division, have made even the eyes of Manchester United water with the money they have forked out in transfer fees and players' wages. They have twice smashed the British record for transfer fees by paying £3 million for Alan Shearer and £5 million for Chris Sutton. They regained their place in the top flight in 1992, after an absence of 26 years – and, of course, followed this up in 1995 by winning the Championship for the first time since 1914.

The other reason why Walker's popularity is difficult for the rest to match concerns his image, which was vividly encapsulated by the sight of his celebrating the clinching of the title with a club scarf around his neck and tears in his eyes.

Referred to as 'Uncle Jack', Walker, for all his wealth, is a man of simple tastes and homespun philosophies. He fights shy of full media interviews – he has been known to give only one – but those who have got close to him talk glowingly of his lack of pretentiousness and his refusal to allow himself to forget his working-class roots. Indeed, he takes delight in reminding himself of them. In the company of the Blackburn players, for example, he is fond of challenging all-comers to the coin-flicking game similar to tiddlywinks that he mastered on the pavements of Blackburn's streets when he was a boy. His pride in his background also comes through in his recollections of the places in the town that featured prominently in his life there. 'You will find out all about the history of Blackburn, and his own business and personal background in the town, when he's driving you through it in his car,' says Rovers manager Ray Harford.

Unlike Sugar and Co, Walker, though having a controlling interest in Blackburn's shares, is not the club's chairman nor even on the board; the fact that he is a resident of the tax-haven of Jersey precludes him from taking up any directorships in the United Kingdom. So his style and title is Blackburn vice-president.

It is tempting to paint a picture of Jack Walker as an eccentric Fairy Godfather – the giant-size version of far less wealthy figures who have subsidised clubs out of the goodness of their hearts without getting anywhere near the same credit for it as him. One of the most disarming examples of this could be found in Scotland, where the small, frail figure of the late John 'Jake' Dalziel, the head of a long-established family bakery business in Airdrie, directed what some might have considered an obsessional amount of generosity towards his local league club – the north of the border equivalent of Wimbledon.

Like Walker, Dalziel shunned personal publicity and was never Airdrie's chairman; until his death in 1993, at the age of 74, he was a member of the board and the club's honorary president. He was an ailing man, his speech and movement having been restricted in the last few years of his life by a series of strokes; but his devotion to Airdrie never wavered.

Some, however, felt that Dalziel's willingness to dig into his own pocket to provide funds for transfers and ground improvements reached the stage at which he needed to be saved from himself. Among these was his son John, who assumed control of the business from his father in May 1987, and who, significantly, took a rather more hard-headed, dispassionate view of the club's financial needs. Dalziel senior, however, continued to open up his heart, and his wallet, to his beloved Airdrie. It was largely due to his support through interest-free loans that they were able to spend more in the transfer market than other First Division clubs at that time, and go full time. Dalziel at least was able to go to that directors' box in the sky with happy memories such as Airdrie's promotion to the Premier Division in 1980 and their Scottish Cup final appearance against Rangers in 1992.

It would appear on the surface that Dalziel and Jack Walker share the same 'weakness', but we should not be misled by this. For instance, Walker has the final say on any transfer deals involving his money and, therefore, it is no coincidence that Blackburn have never paid large transfer fees for players in their late 20s. This is due to the sound Walker business logic concerning the resaleable value of his players; the fact is that if they are down on the balance-sheet as assets (which they are), it hardly makes good investment sense to be stuck in a grave negative equity situation with them when the club decide to part with them. It was partly through this consideration that Rovers, having shown an interest in signing David Platt from Sampdoria in the summer of 1995, didn't put up a fight when Arsenal offered £5 million for him instead.

You suspect that Walker and his counterparts are still haunted by the memories of how the top clubs caught a financial cold – indeed, double pneumonia – in the 1970s and 1980s by allowing themselves to be swept along by their managers' dreams of football grandeur. One club who suffered particularly were Manchester City when they were under the uninhibited management of Malcolm Allison. Even today, any discussion on England's biggest transfer-market boobs comes around sooner or later to City's embarrassment over paying a British record fee of £1.437 million for Steve Daley from Wolves in September 1979, and having to sell him for just £300,000 to Seattle Sounders 15 months later. When clubs find themselves on that slippery slope, it is difficult to halt the decline. In 1996, City were reportedly £19 million in debt.

It is unlikely that Walker will ever find himself in that situation. As Blackburn's chairman, Robert Coar, has said: 'Jack Walker is a businessman, and everything he does is done as if he is running a business. You cannot run a business like a fan.' This, indeed, brings us to the essence of today's leading chairmen, men liable to have not merely businesses, but national and international business empires.

While highlighting the Premiership clubs with links to the Conservative Party, *Labour Research* magazine, in a study of the game's backers and their business interests in August 1995, revealed that Blackburn were one of a number of Premiership clubs which are subsidiaries of other companies, and one of a handful whose parent companies are based abroad. According to the report, ownership of Blackburn – more specifically Walker's ownership of Blackburn – resided in his Channel Island company, Rosedale (JW) Investments. Peter Johnson's majority shareholding in Everton could also be found in a Channel Island company, AIB Trust (Jersey) Ltd. Examples of home-based parent companies included those of Newcastle (a subsidiary of Hall's Cameron Development) and QPR (then a subsidiary of their chairman Richard Thompson's family property investment and construction empire, Thompson Investments).

Moreover, an increasing number of these men have their sights set on following the lead of Manchester United, Tottenham Hotspur and Millwall by turning their clubs into full public limited companies, or that of Chelsea, Celtic and Preston in getting them on the Alternative Investment Market. The amount of personal energy they are devoting to that ultimate power-game target varies. Johnson, for one, told me he was sensitive about giving the impression of 'taking my eye off the ball' in his other business. 'I do run a public company [Park Foods] so I have to be very careful about the image I portray to the City,' he said. So much so that when our discussion at Goodison was interrupted by a member of his secretarial staff asking us if he wanted coffee, and how we took it, he pointed out: 'Now that's an indication that I don't spend much time here. They don't know what coffee I drink or whether I take sugar.'

Not that Johnson remains too much in the Goodison background. 'I am pretty "hands-on",' he conceded. 'One of the things I believe football clubs need is one man with the power to make decisions – a club owner. Boards of directors can be very faceless; in the sense of giving a club direction, they can be a hotch-potch, really. So clubs do need a figurehead, one person that everybody can relate to. When I went up to Glasgow to talk to the Rangers chairman David Murray [in connection with Rangers players Duncan Ferguson and Ian Durrant moving to Everton], he summed it up perfectly when he said: "I do like talking and negotiating with owner-occupiers."

'But I am a good delegator. I do let people get on with their jobs – I'm not poking my nose into everything – and I let all the people concerned have their say before I make a decision.' He pauses, and adds: 'I think I am an autocratic democrat. Is that right?'

Some chairmen are more hands-on than others. A number have their own offices at the clubs, and spend most of their time there. Some even employ themselves. According to a report by financial journalist Alex Spillius in The Observer in May 1995, those paid for their services in 1993–94, the last year of accounts available from all clubs, included Ken Bates (£64,614), Doug Ellis (£120,000), Sir John Hall (£94,606), Alan Sugar (£50,000) and Manchester United's Professor Roland Smith (£43,000). It's not only the chairmen who can get some remuneration for their football work – Spillius's list included Leeds United's executive director Bill Fotherby (£238,995) and Arsenal's vice-chairman David Dein (£110,219) – and sometimes there are two paid from one club.

Although the Football Association has continued to stick to its one-paid-director-only rule, Spillius pointed out that this could be circumvented if the club was a subsidiary of another company or if the recipient formed a company himself and the money was paid for 'technical services'.

What do they do for their money? Perhaps the most graphic illustration of their influence – and how the game has changed – can be found in the balance-sheets of Manchester United.

In their accounts for 1995, when they competed in the European Champions League, United, with a total staff of around 300, had a turnover of almost £61 million and made a profit (before transfers) of £20 million. The most interesting aspect of this is that gate receipts – boosted by income from no fewer than 182 executive boxes – only accounted for a third of that turnover. Of the rest, £23 million poured into the coffers from the merchandising side of the business, £7.4 million came from sponsorships, £6.8 million from television and £3.4 million from the restaurants, bars and conference suites at Old Trafford.

The centrepiece of United's commercial activities is a gigantic superstore alongside the stadium. It sells all manner of merchandise, from United replica kits to bedspreads, from videos to babies' bibs, and it almost rivals the likes of Marks & Spencer and Woolworth's as a Saturday shopping attraction. This can be hard to take among the professional clubs at the other end of the scale, some of whom would be delighted if the number of people who visit that store came through their gates for matches. One recalls Terry Yorath, as manager of Cardiff, getting into conversation one day with a group of local supporters and being told that they'd spent the previous Saturday at Manchester United. 'Did you enjoy the game?' Yorath enquired. 'Oh, we didn't go to the game,' they replied. 'We went to the superstore.'

Of course, United are a club apart – by far the biggest and most glamorous in England. Apart from their merchandising income, the next best way to appreciate the gap between themselves and the rest is to look at the number of people – more than 150,000 – who visit the Old Trafford museum each year. United are the model which everybody is trying to copy. All their Premiership rivals are going down the same diversification road; that of developing the non-football side of their operations to keep pace with the spiralling costs of players' transfer fees and wages and to ensure that the money injected by their owners is not put quite so much at risk by the vagaries of results and performances by their teams.

One or two chairmen seem to get more of a buzz over what is happening to their club in commercial terms than they do over what is happening on the field. To broach the subject with Doug Ellis, for example, is to invite a fulsome speech peppered with terms such as 'fixed assets' and 'capital expenditure'. He talks proudly about the land he has acquired to improve facilities such as carparking at the already sprawling – and superb – Villa Park stadium; their state-of-the-art training ground complex, on which he has even built a small house for the security men; the four Villa Park restaurants, which are capable of producing a total of 2,000 match-day meals; and the 10,000 visitors who pay for guided tours of this empire each summer.

For their 1995 financial year, Villa's fixed assets (bricks and mortar) were listed at £15.493 million, compared with £6.475 million in 1992 when the Premier League started, and £2.767 million in 1985; their turnover stood at £13 million, compared with £7.463 million in 1992 and £1.975 million in 1985; and their operating profit (before transfer fees) was £3.049 million, compared with £377,000 and £42,000.

Ellis was just putting the finishing touches to his 1995 annual report when I met him. 'Cash at the bank, and in hand, is £4,352,000 as of 31 May,' he said proudly. 'So when you come to jealousy among clubs, very few have got that. I would say that 75 per cent of them are in the red.'

This bottom line is something that concerns all chairmen. When I was a guest of Peter Johnson for Everton's first home match of the 1995–96 season, against Arsenal, it was interesting to note his nervousness before the kick-off as he walked around the ground to inspect the club shops and restaurants that had been built or refurbished during the summer. 'The turnover before I came was about £8 million, and now it's £11 million,' he remarked. 'But we still have some way to go. We are still £6 million or so below the turnovers of other big clubs.'

The tug-of-war between Everton and Manchester United over the outstanding Russian winger, Andrei Kanchelskis, was just one illustration of why this bothered him. United had agreed to sell him to the Merseysiders for £7.5 million but then upped the price when his previous club reminded them of a sell-on clause in his contract entitling them to a percentage of that fee. Thus, with the matter due to be resolved immediately after the Arsenal match, Johnson's stroll around the ground before the kick-off was repeatedly punctuated by fans stopping him and asking: 'Are we going to get Kanchelskis, Mr Johnson?'

'It is almost certain we will,' he reassured them. Later, with Everton having lost 2–0, and Johnson's fellow Everton and Park Foods director Clifford Finch attempting to resolve the Kanchelskis problem with United representatives on the telephone, Johnson talked about the pressure on him to conclude the deal.

'It's nothing to do with ego,' he confided. 'What you have to take on board is the pressure that 60,000 fans can put on you. They want these players and they don't care how much we have to pay for them. The transfer fees and the fact that these players earn more in a week than many of them earn in a year doesn't bother them. At Tranmere, the supporters would ask: "Why are you letting that player go?" and I'd have to say: "We can't afford to pay him what he thinks he is worth, and if he thinks he can get it, he has to go elsewhere." To Everton fans, there can be no excuse for that happening at Goodison Park.'

He drew my attention to Everton's unsuccessful attempt to sign Stan Collymore from Nottingham Forest. Everton and Liverpool were the only clubs prepared to pay the then British record £8.5 million transfer fee that Forest wanted for him and Johnson claimed that the personal financial package offered to Collymore was more attractive than the one Liverpool dangled before the striker. Liverpool won the day, Johnson argued, because of circumstances beyond his control – Liverpool's superior record of success and Collymore's friendship with the Liverpool players he had met as a member of the England squad. Hence his determination to land Kanchelskis, which he did;

and to develop Everton's fortunes off the field as well as on it.

In so doing, it would be naïve to think that he – and any other club chairman in his position – would not be boosting his own fortunes as well.

There can be a number of tax advantages in owning a football club, and especially one that is a subsidiary of another company. When a club comes under the umbrella of a holding company, profits and losses can be juggled around within the group. Among the other advantages is that a club in such a set-up is not subject to FA regulations concerning the number of paid directors and, in the event of it going public, the 7.5 per cent limit on the dividends it can pay to shareholders.

Moreover, it is hardly unknown for a chairman or club owner to sell his shares for a higher price than he paid for them. This is where the prospect of clubs becoming public limited companies, enabling their fans to buy a stake in them and thus giving those clubs a fresh cash transfusion, really becomes mind-boggling.

Some chairmen have mixed feelings about the idea. Arsenal's Peter Hill-Wood, one of the few who belong to the old school of club figureheads, has said: 'I don't think it is right. I don't believe a football club should be sold to the general public as an investment. Okay, we at Arsenal have X number of shareholders. But those people basically have shares because they are supporters. It's not an investment. We don't pay a dividend. Arsenal will always be a football club. It is what we set out to be and what we should remain.' For a number of others, however – and especially those who, unlike Hill-Wood, have a controlling interest in their clubs – the example of Manchester United and Martin Edwards represents the ultimate goal. Edwards, a tall, quiet, self-contained 52-year-old, inherited 16 per cent of the club from his late father, the former United chairman Louis Edwards, whom he succeeded in the Old Trafford chair in 1980. Having spent hundreds of thousands of pounds to build up his stake to more than 50 per cent, Edwards picked up several million when he reduced his shareholding to 28 per cent on flotation in 1991. What his remaining shares are worth now must cause Edwards to break out in a cold sweat over the memory of his attempt to sell his entire stockholding to Michael Knighton for £10 million in 1989; a deal which foundered, amidst the most embarrassing of public airings, through Knighton's struggle to come up with the money. At that time, Edwards was reportedly attempting to get 30p a share. Their plc status, and remarkable financial growth – stimulated in no small measure, it has to be stressed, by Edwards' expertise as chief executive – has seen the share value increase almost tenfold.

For the pre-flotation season, United, who desperately needed around £10 million to implement the ground safety recommendations of the Taylor Report, announced an overall loss of £5 million. The flotation raised £16.5 million, and the rest is history.

Not surprisingly, it is a lesson that has captured the imagination of United's closest rivals, especially after reports on 2 April 1996 that the value of Sugar's shares in Tottenham had risen as high as £26 million, three times what he paid for them; and estimates that Edwards and his family had raked in a total of around £30 million from the sale of their United shares but still had £55 million worth left.

Scholar, who spearheaded Tottenham's flotation and who, according to press reports, made a £1 million profit on his Spurs shares when he sold them to Sugar, gives a hypothetical example of how any of today's leading chairmen can hit the jackpot: 'Say Manchester United have a market capitalisation of £200 million [which they have]. Right, Peter Johnson, who put £10 million into Everton, says to himself: "If I can build Everton up to half the size of United, the company would be worth £100 million and my shareholding in it would be worth more than £50 million." What's wrong with that?

'People go into business to make money,' Scholar adds. 'That's what business is about. People would not be putting money into businesses – especially the sort of money people are putting into football clubs – if they did not feel it would be worth more in the future.'

The trend has not gone unnoticed in the media. Among the men

33

who have made the business side of sport their specialist subject is Mihir Bose of the *Daily Telegraph*. Bose, a Tottenham fan, assisted Scholar with his book. He is the author of a weekly column which probes the financial side of the game with a depth and expertise that some chairmen and club owners find uncomfortable. Typical of his investigative doggedness concerning the financial intricacies of clubs, and what those in charge can earn from them, was an article he wrote on Leeds United in March 1996 prior to their takeover by the Caspian Leisure Group: 'The controversial restructuring last August meant that the football club is now owned by a holding company where three directors – Leslie Silver, the chairman, Peter Gilman, the vice-chairman, and Bill Fotherby, the managing director – own almost 98 per cent of the shares. The financial restructuring promises to do well for Silver, Gilman and Fotherby. In 1992, when they took what were called management shares, these shares had a nominal value of £1, and Gilman, Fotherby and Silver each held £35,000 worth of such shares. As a result of August's restructuring, each £1 management share acquired a face value of £186, and the three men's holdings are now worth £6.5 million each.

Bose quoted Gilman saying that his was 'fair' and a just 'reward' for the risks he and Silver had taken in guaranteeing £7 million of Leeds' bank loans. Bose added: 'Fotherby and Gilman have done well during the directorships of Leeds United. Last year, Fotherby received a remuneration of £244,098, making him one of the highest-paid directors in football. Two years ago, Leeds bought a house from him for £265,000. In the last three years, GMI Construction Group, a company in which Gilman has a significant interest, has received contracts from Leeds of over £7.5 million.'

Bose stresses that there has been nothing untoward in any of this. 'But let it not be said,' he argues, 'that being a football director is a thankless job.'

One positive aspect of their greater involvement for the fans – apart from the magnificent stadiums in which they are now watching matches – is the money the top clubs have been spending on securing the best players, especially those from abroad. Many believe that the prices chairmen have been prepared to pay for the top stars, in transfer fees and especially wages have reached farcical proportions. Transfer market spending by Premier League clubs in the 1995 close season totalled £68 million, breaking the previous record by some £22 million, and £80 million in the 1996 close season.

But there is method in some chairmen's apparent transfer market madness. One advantage of the clubs going for big names is that it makes them more attractive to television companies. 'The attraction to BSkyB is one thing, but there is also a lot of TV money when you qualify for the European Champions League, or the Cup-Winners Cup or UEFA Cup,' says Scholar. 'For the two latter competitions, English clubs hold the TV rights for their home ties, which means they can also sell them abroad. If Liverpool, say, draw Sampdoria in the UEFA Cup, they can sell the live coverage to Italy. So, the more internationally known players a club have, the better.'

Richard Halstead, the associate editor of *Business Age* magazine, points out: 'Look at the difference the signing of Jürgen Klinsmann made to Tottenham at a time when they were facing the problems of being banned from the FA Cup and having to start the Premiership season with a 12-point deficit [the initial punishment meted out to them by the FA over alleged irregular payment to players under the pre-Sugar régime].

'The Klinsmann signing obviously had a big effect on season-ticket sales and gate receipts, but this was only the tip of the iceberg. Because their televised matches were so much more attractive with him in the team, they were able to obtain more revenue from ground advertising and so on. It showed the City how the game could work as a business.

'Unlike clubs which are private limited companies, plcs are not allowed to classify their players as fully valued assets. Instead of putting them down for what you have paid for them, you have to depreciate them. In any event, the value of players is unpredictable; they can lose form, get injured or whatever, so the City is more concerned with a club's fixed assets, the things about a club that are steady and can be relied upon.

'However, the impact of Klinsmann at Tottenham was a bit of an eye-opener. Their share prices increased considerably during his season at White Hart Lane. Before he came to Tottenham, their market capitalisation was about £12 million. By the time he left, it was £27 million.'

The message in all this is that Premiership clubs, in striving to follow Manchester United's lead, must have at least one big star attraction on the field. United, of course, have Eric Cantona, whose replica No. 7 shirt is the most popular item in their burgeoning club shops. As the City is less concerned with trophies and stylish football than it is with profit margins, it is perhaps not surprising that United resisted the pressure to sell the Frenchman following the infamous kung-fu attack on a Crystal Palace supporter that led to his eight-month suspension from the game in the 1994–95 season.

The insatiable desire of chairmen to buy footballers with some measure of charisma is certainly benefiting the players, not to mention their agents. The European Union ruling in the Jean-Marc Bosman case – that a club can no longer demand a transfer fee when a player has reached the end of his contract – is going to put more money than ever in the performers' pockets. Moreover, one prominent agent reckons that players will become virtually walking billboards, with those at the top of the attraction-factor list earning many times more from advertising and endorsements than they will from playing football. In that eventuality, the relationship between them and their club employers is likely to be even closer than their relationship with their team managers, many of whom have already found themselves becoming marginalised as their clubs have got bigger and more eclectic in their income sources.

But is all this as good for the game as one might think? How long, for example, will fans be happy to pay increased ticket prices and to put up with clubs exploiting the appeal among youngsters for replica kits by repeatedly changing the designs and colours of their playing strips? How long will the fans be able to ignore the feeling that the chairmen are putting the interests of television before the interests of the potential audience for matches at the stadiums? There have already been clear signs of supporters' discontent on that score, if only because of the manner in which the demands of TV have caused so many Saturday match programmes – and the leading competitions – to become fragmented and confusing.

Football is fortunate at the moment in that it is in vogue. Once referred to as the 'working man's ballet', the game now appeals to a much wider range of socio-economic groups, including a greater percentage of women. In helping to take the game 'up-market', however, the chairmen also stand accused of taking it away from its most loyal support base.

It is interesting to listen to Scholar and Halstead on this subject. Scholar, arguably one of the most commercially orientated and innovative of all the top chairmen when he was at Spurs, has this to say: 'The fan who used to stand on the terrace will say: "Ah well, clubs are only interested in the people who want to spend the most money; the people who buy executive boxes etc," but that's not true. Clubs are interested in anybody who comes to the game. It is not cheap to watch football, but nor is it cheap to do a lot of other things. Tottenham's season-ticket prices, for example, doubled in the ten years that I was there. Against that, you look at the rate of inflation, and the extent to which people's pay packets and disposable income has gone up. People's living standards have changed enormously in the last 20 or 25 years. You think about it.

'I have problems with the view that football has gone up-market. Do the people who say that mean that football has suddenly found a whole new audience of people who previously hadn't been to a game in their lives? There might be some cases to support this – you know, youngsters might have taken their fathers along to a match and their fathers have suddenly thought: "Oh, I like this." But, generally, the new audiences are people who wanted to go to football matches but were put off by the poor stadium facilities and crowd violence.

'As for the commercial aspects of the game, the unfortunate thing is that people don't like progress. It reminds me a little bit of my father. When colour television came along, we were driving him mad to get a set. "Come on, let's get colour TV," we'd say. "No. Who needs colour TV – we've got black and white," he'd argue. However, when we eventually did get one, he was telling us how fantastic it was and what a great idea it was to get it.'

Halstead looks at the situation in English football a little differently: 'Commercialism cannot be avoided – it is inevitable – but the big questions for football are what level of commercialism does it really want, and how can it go wrong? Football clubs are very lucky in that they have such a loyal customer base. Even the Marks & Spencer customer base isn't as loyal as that of clubs such as Manchester United and Newcastle. The potential mistake for football is to say to itself: "We've got a unique product, so we can charge what we like for it and do what we like with it." Now, 25 years ago, the market would buy that – most of the people who went to grounds were happy just to see a match. But, with football having attracted middle-income groups, the market for the game is now much more sophisticated and variable. Many of these people don't have the same emotional links with football as the traditional hard-core supporters. They go to football to have a good day out, but they could just as easily switch on to something else.'

If that were to happen, would those who have been squeezed out of going to live matches – and who have become used to watching the game on TV – want to come back?

In that respect, if there's one particularly poignant summing up of how the men who run the clubs nowadays have changed the game, it is that of Keith Burkinshaw, Tottenham's manager when Irving Scholar took over the club. Burkinshaw, a dyed-in-the-wool football professional if ever there was one, found it difficult to come to terms with Scholar's progressive ideas and methods. At the inevitable parting of the ways, Burkinshaw just shook his head sadly and remarked: 'There used to be a football club here.'

TWO

Chairmen 1, Managers 0

Life was good for Keith Burkinshaw at Tottenham before Irving Scholar, a chairman who could be described as the trail-blazer for his counterparts today, arrived on the White Hart Lane scene in 1982.

With two FA Cup triumphs in successive years under his belt, and with his public image having been enhanced by the impact of his innovatory 1976 Argentinian World Cup signings, Ossie Ardiles and Ricardo Villa, this typically down-to-earth south Yorkshireman – solid, dependable and honest to a fault – had come a long way since starting his working life transporting tubs of coal from the pit face at Dodworth Colliery.

In his football career, too, the role of being the manager of a club of Tottenham's stature and glitter represented a giant leap forward. As a player, Burkinshaw's only experience of that sort of glamour came at the very beginning of his 15-year career, with four years as a wing-half on Liverpool's books. But he made only one first-team appearance at Anfield, and the rest of his playing days were spent at Workington and Scunthorpe in the lower divisions. When he retired from playing in 1968, his low-profile career was immediately maintained on the coaching side through a job in Zambia, and again when he was brought to Newcastle as reserve-team coach by United manager Joe Harvey, who had worked with him at Workington.

Harvey, an outstanding motivator, promoted him to first-team coach, and Burkinshaw, who was able to complement Harvey perfectly through his greater technical knowledge of the game and more pragmatic approach, justified the decision by helping to steer Newcastle to the 1974 FA Cup final. It was to be the same story at Tottenham.

Controversially sacked by Newcastle amid the management reshuffle which saw Harvey become general manager at St James' Park in 1975, Burkinshaw joined Spurs as assistant to Terry Neill, taking over from Neill as manager 12 months later. The appointment was not greeted with universal enthusiasm by Tottenham fans. Apart from his undistinguished background in the game, Burkinshaw's experience of being in the number-one team management position had been limited to one short spell as player-manager of Workington, and another as caretaker manager of Scunthorpe. Not surprisingly, the misgivings among the Tottenham faithful intensified when Spurs were relegated in his first season. Certainly, nobody then can have envisaged his becoming the second most successful manager in Tottenham's history, behind his fellow Yorkshireman Bill Nicholson – even with Nicholson having been brought back onto the club's staff by Burkinshaw.

But the one thing the Yorkshireman had going for him, apart from his steely character, was his popularity among the players. In addition to his knowledge of the game, his straightforwardness as a person – though bordering occasionally on bluntness – made him a manager they could trust. There were no airs and graces about Burkinshaw. He was totally dedicated to the game, and to upholding the simple, straightforward principles with which he had been brought up.

Those principles, forged at a time when boys would spend countless hours practising their skills in the streets, when all professional players earned the same amount and had a close affinity with their local communities, did not make it easy for him to adjust to the changes in attitude following the abolition of the maximum wage. But it says much about his influence on some of the rich cats at Tottenham that when Glenn Hoddle started his own managerial career at Swindon, he appointed Burkinshaw onto his backroom staff; and that Ardiles did likewise when he became West Bromwich Albion's manager.

To those players who considered themselves stars deserving preferential treatment – or those elegant, strolling types whose performances were perceived by Burkinshaw as being worthy only of receiving marks for artistic merit – he was not a man to be taken lightly.

Malcolm Macdonald, the swashbuckling England centre-forward who was Newcastle's most fêted player when Burkinshaw was at the club, says: 'He is one of the coaches with whom I had the most disagreements. He is an extremely intelligent man who can converse on most topics, and I got on very well with him as a person. But it was different in our football relationship. He used to get so frustrated with me because I would not do what he wanted with regards to contributing to the team's general play. All I was interested in was scoring goals.

'We used to have some terrible rows over it – unbelievable rows. One, I recall, took place in this cricket pavilion, which had a pillar or column in the middle of it. We started off arguing about something as we were walking across the room, and the more heated the argument became, the closer we got to each other. In the end, it was only the pillar which kept us apart. I am convinced that had it not been there, we would have ended up fighting each other on the floor. It would have been some fight as well, because Keith was as hard as they come.'

Burkinshaw later showed both his stubbornness in sticking to what he believed in, and his lack of tact, through his bust-up at Tottenham with another centre-forward, Steve Archibald. It all began in a match against Coventry early in the 1983–84 season, when Archibald, whose strong-mindedness and laid-back style did not make him one of Burkinshaw's favourite players, signalled to the bench that he had sustained an injury and wanted to be substituted. Burkinshaw, though, felt that Archibald could easily have carried on and virtually accused the Scottish international of cheating. Archibald refused to talk to Burkinshaw again unless the manager gave him a public apology. The apology was not forthcoming, however, and the embarrassing rift between the two men – while Archibald continued as a key member of Burkinshaw's team – grew ever wider.

According to Irving Scholar, the pressure this put on the pair affected Burkinshaw rather more than it did Archibald, and the episode spelled the beginning of the end for him at Spurs. In truth, the beginning of the end for Burkinshaw came when Scholar took over the club, if only because of the culture clash it produced between these two vastly different characters. It was a clash that many managers of Burkinshaw's generation have got to appreciate exceptionally well.

One of the major changes in the game in recent years, insofar as managers are concerned, is that they have lost some of their power and influence. The extent to which this has happened varies from club to club, and from chairman to chairman. But while the successful team managers used to dominate almost every aspect of their clubs, it is fair to say that they have been cut down to size in recent years. The more the game has grown as a business, with clubs having a greater number of ways of generating income, the more these men have been marginalised.

The latest example of this trend in England came at Chelsea, when Glenn Hoddle left the club at the end of the 1995–96 season to become Terry Venables' successor as England coach, and Ruud Gullit took over from him at Stamford Bridge as player-manager. It was important to Chelsea, and to Gullit, that the Dutch master could continue to give of his best as a player. Thus, to ensure that every management gap would be filled, the club promoted Graham Rix from youth-team coach to first-team coach; Colin Hutchison, the club's chief executive, was put in charge of all transfer and contract negotiations; and Gwyn Williams, who like Rix had been on the coaching staff, stepped into the position of administrative manager.

It was stressed that Gullit would only be responsible for the selection of players for the first team and first-team performances and results. Ken Bates put it this way: 'You would not expect Ruud to go to Peterborough on a wet Tuesday night to watch a player we fancy. Player-manager is an impossible job, so we have built a fence around him.'

But even for non-playing managers, this is the way things have been done on the Continent for a number of years. In other countries, 'managers' are basically 'coaches'; and the terms of reference of their jobs have been nothing like as wide-ranging as they have been for their British counterparts. For example, a coach on the Continent is only responsible for training, coaching and team selection; all financial decisions and negotiations relating to transfer fees and the salaries and bonuses of their players are the responsibility of the club president.

Ironically, Keith Burkinshaw had first-hand experience of this himself through a post-Tottenham spell as coach at Sporting Lisbon: 'I asked the president: "How can you decide how much a player is worth? Are you saying that you are an expert on football and footballers?" He looked at me as if I was mad.'

Such is the coach's place in the scheme of things on the Continent that it has not been unknown for a president to buy a player and then present the signing to the coach as a *fait accompli*. No British club chairman would admit to usurping his manager's authority in this way. Nonetheless, when you raise the subject, some chairmen do tend to leave you with the impression that they feel establishing a successful football team – or some aspects of it at least – is not quite the specialist art that managers claim it is; indeed, there is even the suggestion that managers have created something of a myth about their roles.

The fact that a lot of chairmen occasionally reveal themselves as frustrated managers, if not players, has always been the case. 'Like every fan at every game, they can all pick a better team and name better players to buy,' Scholar points out. Another thing which hasn't changed is the paranoia a manager feels when his chairman asks him to explain his methods and then voices opinions on them. It is clearly possible to find a middle ground in all this; but because of the assertiveness of the men in control of the big clubs, and their determination to run them on sound business principles, the dividing line has inevitably become more blurred.

Chairmen argue, not unreasonably, that the financial side of the game has become too big and too complex for managers to cope with; and that, having poured so much money into their clubs, they have every right to protect and develop their investments in any way they deem necessary.

There is also the question of the temptations placed in a manager's path in major transfer deals, especially when those deals are conducted through an agent. The point was brought into sharp focus by the George Graham 'bungs' scandal at Arsenal, which led to Graham's dismissal by the club, a 12-month FA ban and the promise by Arsenal that never again would a manager of theirs be allowed so much responsibility.

Nobody would ever suggest that someone like Burkinshaw would capitalise on his position in this way, least of all Scholar. Nonetheless, when you consider the different worlds the two men inhabited – and their contrasting views on the direction in which the top clubs and English football should be heading – it is not difficult to appreciate why theirs was a marriage which was never going to last.

At a time when most club chairmen were old enough to be the players' grandfathers, Scholar was only 36 – some 13 years younger than Burkinshaw – when he took the chair at White Hart Lane. A personable, likeable man whose enthusiasm for Tottenham and football knew no bounds, he was as progressive and imaginative as Burkinshaw was conservative and pragmatic.

Among the first things Scholar did on assuming control of Tottenham was to take the club's commercial manager on a trip to the United States to study marketing techniques in that country. Among the other initiatives which raised the eyebrows of some of his more staid counterparts at other clubs was the hiring of Saatchi and Saatchi for a Tottenham match advertising campaign. Some of his ideas were better than others. Under his command, for example, Tottenham were the first club to introduce a 'Dial-a-Seat' telephone credit card booking system; and the first to grade the prices of league matches in accordance with the demand to see the games.

'With most of the things we did, a lot of people in the game would say: "Oh, that won't work." But we'd stick our heads above the parapet and at least try it.' He shrugs, and adds: 'They weren't fantastic ideas as far as I was concerned – just commonsense things that people didn't seem to think about. I am not knocking these people; I think that when you are in the game for a long time it can get to the stage where you can't see the wood for the trees sometimes.'

The same could be said for many Spurs fans, especially when Scholar, forced to restructure the East Stand to comply with safety regulations (at a cost of some £2 million, not to mention a reduction in the stand's capacity), came up with plans to replace its famous middle-tier standing area – the 'Shelf' – with 36 executive boxes. The argument that Tottenham were short of money and that the boxes, though costing £1.5 million, would produce an invaluable income of £750,000 a year, counted for little among the White Hart Lane diehards who saw it as yet another step towards turning Tottenham into a club for Yuppies. The outcry was such that Scholar, himself a Shelf spectator once, revised his plans by turning it into a standing season-ticket area.

In most other things, however, Scholar would not allow tradition to blind him to the 'inevitability of change and progress'. It is perhaps typical of the man that, far from being impressed by the wave of commercialism that has engulfed English football since he first bathed Tottenham in it, he does not believe that the clubs have exploited the potential as much as they could – indeed should – have done.

This view would not go down too well with those fans who complain about being 'ripped off' by clubs, especially with regards to the number of times that clubs change their kit to exploit the replica strip market. Ironically, Manchester United, who are reckoned to be the biggest culprits, got their comeuppance on the field in season 1995–96 when their contract with Umbro forced them to use their second-choice grey strip for the Premiership match against Southampton at The Dell. United conceded three goals in the first 45 minutes and at half-time manager Alex Ferguson, claiming that it had been difficult for the players to pick each other out in their dull garb, ordered a switch to their third-choice blue strip for the second half. 'Enough is enough,' muttered Ferguson, referring to the demands of United's commercial operation.

Scholar, though, says, 'Football shirts have become big fashion items. As far as the kids are concerned, they are good value for money, too, because the kids are wearing them morning, noon and night. Every season, a newspaper will say: "Oh, the clubs are changing their strips again – they are exploiting the fans." But it's supply and demand.' In that context, he has nothing but praise for the example set by Manchester United: 'All clubs had merchandising operations when I was at Tottenham – they all had their club shops – but they did not see it as an integral part of their business. I don't think they see it as an integral part of their business today either. The only exception is Manchester United because they manufacture and produce things themselves.

'That's what we did. I had seen merchandising in America – the fact that you couldn't go into a single sports shop in the entire United States without seeing American gridiron, baseball and basketball products. It had spread to this country. Kids were walking around England with New York Yankees T-shirts, New York Yankees bomber jackets. I thought: "What the hell is going on? We've got our own national sport, and the kids should be wearing the products of Spurs and Arsenal and so on." When I first went to Spurs, the merchandising division was raking in something like £300,000 a year; by the time I left, it was up to about £3 million. The reason is that we did not buy all the products from wholesalers and people like that; instead, wherever possible, we tried to cut out the middle man. I'll give you an example. Say you went along to

Liverpool today and said: "I want to write a book about Liverpool – can I make it official?" You offer to give the club X amount, and they say: "Fine – go ahead." Now, you're writing an official Liverpool book, endorsed by the club. Why shouldn't they be the ones to take charge of it? Why shouldn't they be the ones to pay you X amount for writing it, and publish it themselves?

'As I said, Manchester United have this approach, and it's down to a man called Edward Freeman [whom Scholar brought to Tottenham as their merchandising supremo]. When he went to Old Trafford, their merchandising turnover was just under £2 million; within three years, it was approaching 12 times that. Don't tell me that it's only because it's Manchester United – I don't think that is true. It's because he has approached it as a business; he and they have taken it more seriously than the rest.'

When it came to taking things seriously himself, Scholar was equally assertive and progressive on political issues relating to English football as a whole. On subjects he cared about – and no subject absorbed him quite like the backward thinking of English football – the animated Scholar was inexhaustible. He was nothing if not engaging – and persuasive. As he says: 'Jack Dunnett [then the Football League president] used to laugh, and say: "You put up more proposals for regulation changes than anybody else, and I tell you what, you don't do badly – you get half of them through."

'I found that the trick was to put up two or three variations to a proposal so that all the objections that the chairmen might have to it would be covered and that they would be forced to discuss it properly – and hopefully see the merits in it – rather than dismiss it out of hand.

'There were so many things that struck me as being archaic. I heard something that frightened the life out of me: I was told that the manager of a First Division club had rung his chairman to tell him that he'd signed a player for £900,000 off his own bat, and that the chairman had replied: "Where do you think we're going to get the money from? We haven't got the money." The chairman had to call an emergency board meeting that night, and ended up having to stump up the money himself. At one of the chairmen's meetings, I said: "Do you realise that, as the regulations stand at the moment, your manager can go out and sign whoever he wants, and you are on the hook?" Well, you should have seen their reaction. So I put up a regulation that any transfer document and player's contract had to be countersigned by at least two top club officials; that is, two directors, or the chairman and the secretary.'

This was by no means the only area in which Scholar's boardroom counterparts – at least those at top level – had good cause to be grateful for his presence. He was no longer involved with the game at the time his fellow chairmen took the giant steps towards formalising the Premier League and, equally important, landing the television deal from BSkyB that for a number of chairmen had seemed beyond their wildest dreams. Nonetheless, it is Scholar, through his vision and remarkable energy as an agitator for radical change, who is generally credited as having done as much as anyone in attaining these targets.

The irony is that he himself has mixed feelings about such developments. He is a great believer in the pyramid league system in other countries – and the argument that the sum total of the old Football League was greater than its individual parts. As for the BSkyB deal, he complains that the club chairmen were too easily influenced by the £42 million difference between the BSkyB and ITV offers, and did not pay enough attention to factors such as BSkyB paying half the rate per match that ITV offered; BSkyB's comparatively limited number of viewers, a potential drawback in the clubs' efforts to maximise their ground advertising and sponsorship revenue; and the possibility of BSkyB's 60-matches-per-season schedule taking live coverage of the game to the extreme.

'The chairmen took the money and that was it. That's football's unfortunate weakness – it is too easy to take the money on offer without actually thinking. Did anyone sit down and think about what the deal was worth to BSkyB? No one. Also, when the deal was signed, BSkyB made no mention whatsoever that they were going to show the matches on a subscription basis – everybody thought that viewers were going to be able to watch the games for nothing. The Premier League clubs should have had a cut of the subscriptions.'

As the head of one of the so-called 'Big Five' clubs of English football – the others then were Arsenal, Manchester United, Liverpool and Everton – Scholar felt that such clubs were being held back by the voting structure in the Football League, that the tail too often wagged the dog when it came to First Division clubs attempting to push through changes that would benefit them, and that the first Division clubs did not get a big enough share of the Football League television and sponsorship income. For example, nothing rankled with him more than the fact that the income from TV in those days (a paltry sum compared to what it is now because ITV and BBC had the field to themselves and operated a cartel to force football to accept whatever they offered) had to be shared equally among all 92 clubs. To him, it was unacceptable that a club like Hartlepool, who had not had any matches televised in a season, should receive the same amount – £25,000 – as Manchester United, who had been on the box 18 times.

Such anomalies had long bothered the top clubs. But with Scholar and the similarly gung-ho Arsenal director David Dein happy to throw their weight behind the crusade to change matters – and, indeed, lead the others into battle – it was much more than merely brave talk.

The crusade really began to take root in Scholar in the summer of 1983, when Tottenham and Manchester United were involved in a close-season tour of Swaziland. Scholar, who was content at that time to own Tottenham without having a seat on the board, recalls: 'It was the first time I had met Martin Edwards [United's chairman]. Douglas Alexiou [Tottenham's chairman] and I were having dinner with him and one of his directors, and as they were chatting about their problems, I nudged Douglas and said: "They've got the same headaches that we've got," and we started to exchange ideas on how we could solve them.

'For me, it all boiled down to the fact that, while every club has problems, those of a club like Tottenham or Manchester United were different to those of clubs in different divisions. I thought: "Hang on a moment – if clubs in the top flight have similar problems, and we're all like-minded, then really we should be in a position to make decisions that will help ease them.'"

One example of the difficulties Scholar experienced in this concerned his fight to increase the number of match substitutes a team could use from one to two. 'It was my first step in trying to establish a set of rules, within the structure of the Football League, that would benefit the clubs who generated the most income and attention. It was argued against quite strongly by the Third and Fourth Division clubs. Jimmy Hill [then a Charlton director], in particular, stood up and said it would mean that they would have to carry an extra person on the coach, cost them an extra bonus payment – all the little negative things. "We're not all public limited companies, you know," he told me. I turned around and said: "Look, I don't mind if you don't want to do it – let us do it as an experiment, and if it works and you want to follow us, fine. We don't have to make it mandatory." It must have taken me three or four annual general meetings of the Football League to get it squeezed through and approved, and no one since has complained.'

Scholar and his fellow revolutionaries were no less aggressive in their threats to defy the Football League. The first blow-up came in 1985, when the five giants – with Scholar, Dein, Edwards and Everton's Phil Carter at the forefront – announced their intention to form a 'Super League' outside the jurisdiction of the Football League, if the rules were not changed to give them greater power. On that occasion, the walk-out was averted by a six-hour meeting of the clubs at Heathrow on 1 December 1985, and the emergence of a ten-point agreement which included the three-quarters majority necessary for rules changes being reduced to two-thirds; the number of votes for each First Division club being increased from one to one and a half; the First Division being given 50 per cent of the centralised TV and sponsorship income; and a reduction in the number of First Division clubs from 22 to 20.

Three years later, Scholar & Co again emphasised their determination to go it alone if necessary, this time as a result of a carrot dangled before them by ITV. The carrot was produced by Greg Dyke, ITV's controller of sport, when the BSB satellite company – then in rivalry with Rupert Murdoch's Sky – showed an interest in televising matches live. It was an exciting development for the game, not least for men like Scholar who had yearned for another potential buyer in the television market to break the ITV–BBC cartel. However, while most Football League chairmen were in favour of the proposed BSB deal, the Scholar camp were concerned about the lengthy duration of the contract they were being offered – ten years – and BSB's financial position. Scholar himself took the view that, though satellite TV would play an important part in the future of the game, it would be better for English football to sit tight and wait until companies such as BSB had progressed a little further along the development road.

Enter Mr Dyke, and his carrot. The deal he put forward – around £50 million over four years for 20 live matches a season – was bound to appeal to the top clubs because it was set up to benefit them the most. Indeed, Dyke made no bones about the fact that he was only interested in a small number of league clubs. Hence the fact that Manchester United, Tottenham, Arsenal, Liverpool and Everton were left licking their lips over an offer of £1 million each per season (not including appearance fees); and that there was no shortage of clubs queuing up for the privilege of being among the five others for whom Dyke had earmarked £400,000 each a season. The clubs who jumped on the bandwagon – Aston Villa, Newcastle, West Ham, Sheffield Wednesday and Nottingham Forest – did manage to persuade the Big Five to take a slightly smaller slice of the cake. But the more significant aspect of the affair was that the Football League, again facing the possibility of a walk-out by the leading clubs, was forced to capitulate and go along with them. So ITV won the day – and the First Division's income from the money was increased from 50 per cent to 75 per cent.

Little wonder that Dyke has been described as the 'Godfather' of the Premiership. By that criterion, one could say that Scholar and

Dein were among its blood brothers – Dein especially. His part in holding the league to ransom over the 1988 ITV deal did not go down too well with the men in charge of clubs outside the Big Five, which was only to be expected given that he was a member of the Football League management committee and therefore had a mandate to address himself to the best interests of all its members, big or small. Chelsea's Ken Bates and Crystal Palace's Ron Noades, his fellow committee members and two men whose views contrasted sharply with those of Dein on some important issues, took a particularly dim view of his approach. To them, and to many others, it was little short of treachery. They had the same view of Carter, who was chairman of the committee and the Football League president. But it was Dein who received most of the flak. Bates has had some ferocious verbal digs at him in his noted column in Chelsea's match programme, and Noades still carries a copy of the letter that ITV wrote to Dein outlining how Arsenal would benefit from the Big Five offer. Dein's campaign for the deal to be accepted led to his being removed from the committee (as was Carter); and to the unbridled delight of Bates and Noades, Dein was perceived to sustain another blow when BSkyB beat ITV in their battle over the exclusive television rights to the Premiership.

Even today, the mere mention of Dein's name immediately prompts Bates and Noades to turn back the clock to 1988. 'David Dein screwed it up and I'll never forgive him for it,' says Bates in his inimitable over-the-top fashion. The Chelsea man still feels that the proposed BSB contract would have been better for the game as a whole, even though subsequent events have borne out the Big Five's misgivings about it. Ironically, notwithstanding BSB's financial difficulties, which led to their being taken over by Sky, the length of the contract they were seeking would have meant that had it been signed, the Premiership would not have come into existence in 1992. But as Bates says: 'Under the ITV deal, we saw clubs like Arsenal, Tottenham, Manchester United, Liverpool and Everton on the box more often than we saw *Coronation Street*. That gave them the exposure that enabled them to build up a nationwide supporters base, and build up their merchandising and so on.' He stresses that he admires Dein for his determination to get the best deal for his club, but adds: 'It's important that all clubs start on a level playing-field.'

Bates, in fact, got his revenge on Dein – not to mention on Scholar and Edwards – at the Football League AGM in August 1990 when his proposal to return the First Division to 22 clubs was overwhelmingly carried. Only Arsenal, Tottenham and Manchester United, who clung to the view that there should be fewer First Division matches, not more, voted against the proposal. But these three, enviously looking at the way in which other major European leagues were structured to enhance the performances of their biggest clubs and their national team, took the result badly enough to start thinking seriously again of a breakaway.

Scholar recalls: 'The crazy thing about Bates's proposal is that the three clubs who voted against it probably stood to gain as much as anyone from the increase to 22 clubs. The only way the other clubs feel they can sell themselves to the public is by having more and more matches. The bigger clubs are in a different position; they value themselves more highly; their commercial spin-offs are far greater and their pursuit of excellence creates a better product. They do not make the false equation of more matches equalling more money. I felt very unhappy about the change. David Dein, too, felt very strongly that something had to be done, and within a few months he contacted me. He was convinced that, despite the new TV contract and the money being paid to the First Division, the League structure had to change. We needed a new system, one that benefited not only the big clubs but the game itself and the national team. I agreed with that, but warned him that if we were not going to have to dance to the same old music again, to the same old tired routine, we could not merely talk about breakaways. That was hot air.'

In December of that year, Dein and Noel White (then Liverpool's chairman) arbitrarily approached the FA with this idea, an obvious step in view of the fact that it was the FA, not the Football League, which governed English football and which was recognised as such by FIFA and UEFA. The FA, having repeatedly been at loggerheads with the Football League over the years, and ever conscious of the need for a set-up at professional level which would help the England team, gave the pair the green light.

Scholar has enormous respect for Dein, whom he points out is as genuine a fan of Arsenal as he himself has been of Tottenham, and who is very much on the same wavelength as himself on how to propel the major clubs and the game into the modern world. Some insiders argue that Scholar was the easier of the two to like, a reference to the fact that he was more open and out-going to outsiders – and notably the media – and that he was generally regarded as being more adept than Dein at balancing the needs and requirements of his own club with those of the game as a whole.

But there was a considerable emotional and cultural link between the two: born of the same generation, they both come from similar Jewish north London backgrounds. It was rare that Jewish people were attracted to professional football, other than as supporters, and even though Scholar and Dein reached the positions they did at clubs with a strong Jewish following, it seemed at times almost as if they had gatecrashed an exclusive party. To some people in the game, and especially the more traditional and blinkered members of English football's hierarchy, the pair's assertiveness and preoccupation with the commercial aspect of the game encapsulated all the old prejudices against their race.

They certainly personified its reputation for ambitiousness and hard work. 'The work ethic,' Scholar acknowledges. 'You're brought up on that basis – it goes from the cradle to the grave. You work hard, you will achieve something; you don't work hard, you won't achieve anything. It's all about work, work, work.'

At Tottenham, however, Scholar's energy – or rather the channels in which it was directed – was difficult for his manager Keith Burkinshaw to accept and deal with. Quite apart from his ideas on the overall basis on which clubs should be run, Scholar knew more about football than a lot of other club owners – and not just about

English football. As a resident of Monte Carlo, he was a walking, talking encyclopaedia on the international game, including the advantages of managers doing their jobs within the framework of the Continental club system — and of chairmen (or club presidents) being heard as well as seen.

As Scholar says: 'I suggested as long as 13 years ago that this was the way English football was going to go. I could see that the potential was there for the game to attract vast sums of money, and you had to question what experience managers had in dealing with this. As football clubs got bigger, the more they have required to be broken down into departments run by specialists in each particular field.'

Thus, in terms of the guidelines of chairman-manager relationships, Scholar's arrival at White Hart Lane took Burkinshaw from one extreme to another.

Burkinshaw's previous chairmen there had been two men in their 70s: Sidney Wale, an accountant who took over that position from his late father, Fred; and Arthur Richardson. Burkinshaw was particularly fond of Wale. 'He was a great chairman for me,' he recalls. 'He used to come in on the Friday morning to pick up his match tickets for the next day, poke his head around my office door, and say: "Well, Keith, what's going on this week? Anything you want to tell me?" I'd chat with him for a couple of minutes, and then he'd say: "Right, must go — got my tickets to collect." That was all I saw of him. Outside things like ground improvements, he let me and Geoff Jones [then Tottenham's secretary] run the club.

'What you did in those days was that, at the end of the season, you'd have the secretary in and between you you decided how much money could be spent on transfer fees and players' wages, the groundstaff and so on. Everything that was going on at the club, you knew about; and, usually, the chairman was quite happy to rubber-stamp whatever you wanted to do.

'In the past, if you look at all the most successful clubs, I think you would find that the managers made sure things revolved around them. During my time under the chairmanship of Sidney Wale, they brought in a chief executive — a more dynamic figure than Geoff Jones — and everybody had to report to him. There was no way I was going to do that. "Nobody is going to be over me," I said. "I am the strongest person in this club and I'm not reporting to anybody." Sidney Wale said: "Oh, not you — just the others."

'When I think of the faith he showed in me, I always remember the time that, having not been in the job long, I wanted a centre-forward from Ipswich [David Johnson]. I said to Sid Wale: "Look, how much can we afford to spend on new players?" and he said: "X amount." So I told him that I wanted to spend that amount on one player, told him who he was, and asked him if he felt he would like to sit in with me during the negotiations. He wouldn't hear of it. "You have been appointed manager of the club, and we expect you to manage. We have confidence in you — you will do the deal."

'It gave me so much confidence it was unbelievable. I did all the deals when he and Arthur Richardson were in charge. I did the deals that brought Ardiles and Villa to Spurs. Now Ossie, one of the best players in the world, did not get any more than our top-paid players at the time. We were quoted £700,000 and I arranged for the payment to be made in dollars because the rate of exchange was favourable to us and meant a saving of some £35,000 to £40,000. The money included Ossie's signing-on fee, everything. What chairman could have done better than that?

'From day one, the feeling I had about Scholar was that he felt he knew more about football than any manager. He wasn't chairman initially, but when he bought the club he invited me and my wife to Monte Carlo. I always remember him and me sitting together, over-looking the sea. The way the conversation was going, I could tell that he wanted to be involved in all the things I was sort of in charge of. I said: "Look, Irving, if you have any sense, you'll just look at the success Tottenham have achieved in recent seasons and not interfere. When you become chairman, just let me run the show and you can sit back and take all the accolades. I am not being big-headed, but I know that's the best way forward for the club."

'I'm sure that my saying that to him was my death knell. To be fair, at the start of his chairmanship, he did allow me to continue doing what I had been doing before. But, more and more, he started trying to come in on things and I suppose I went the other way with him because I genuinely felt that if I gave him an inch, he would take a mile.'

Burkinshaw feels that he might have given Scholar more than that inch to begin with, simply by encouraging him to accompany Bill Nicholson on his scouting trips in order to improve his appreciation of how the professionals view the game. Scholar himself recalls how much he learned by watching matches alongside Peter Shreeves, then Burkinshaw's assistant, in the White Hart Lane directors' box. 'He'd talk all the way through a game and he opened my eyes enormously to what was really going on out there. Most of us who watch football matches keep our eyes on the ball, what is happening around the ball, but the pros are more concerned about the movement of players in other areas. You know, someone hits a long pass, and you say: "Oh, what a great pass that was." You don't often appreciate the intelligent 40-yard run that another player has made to create the chance for it. These are the things I learned from Bill Nicholson and Peter Shreeves. It was fascinating – I had my eyes opened, like a child.'

On the basis that a little knowledge can be a dangerous thing, however, Burkinshaw would argue that Nicholson and Shreeves have much to answer for. 'One thing that really annoyed me was that Scholar was even talking to players about wages behind my back,' Burkinshaw claims. 'You'd have a player in to discuss a new contract, and he'd say: "Well, you're offering me £30,000 a year but Irving Scholar has already said that he'll give me £40,000." It put me in an impossible position – how can you expect to motivate players if they know you're not the strong figure at the club?'

Scholar looks taken aback when you put all this to him today. He insists that he got on well with Burkinshaw, a view that his manager generally endorses. Nonetheless, Burkinshaw is touchy about a passage in Scholar's book which reads: 'Keith Burkinshaw wanted to be in on every aspect of the club, many of which had absolutely nothing to do with football.' Referring to Burkinshaw's visiting him in the South of France, Scholar added: 'He explained that earlier in his career, he had taken a two-year course in finance and was fully capable of handling this side of the club. How could he have found two whole years to devote to the course? His reply was classic. "It was a course that lasted one week one year and one week the next." As he said it, he guffawed loudly, clearly relishing the joke. I have replayed those words often, and it has made me realise that there is something called truth and then there is managers' truth or soccer-speak. They have a way with words which, whilst they may not be untrue, do not quite mean what we all think they mean.'

During my interview with him, Scholar recalled that when he and Burkinshaw got together in the South of France, he talked to the manager about the methods employed at Liverpool. Scholar had been given to understand that Liverpool managers had become used to concentrating simply on football matters such as coaching and team selection, with the club's chief executive, Peter Robinson, taking some of the pressure off them by handling the financial and administrative aspects of the job. 'I asked Keith whether he agreed that Liverpool provided the model for other clubs to follow, and if he agreed with all their methods, and he said yes. As far as wage negotiations with players were concerned, I was influenced by the views of Bill Nicholson, who actually felt that having to thrash out new deals with players could be a handicap to him. He said: "If I am unable or unwilling to give a player what he has asked for, how can I expect him to want to give me 100 per cent?"'

Burkinshaw, though, was nothing if not set in his ways. One example of the conflict this created between the two men concerned Gary Mabbutt's initial Tottenham contract after the player had been bought from Bristol Rovers. Scholar recalls: 'Mabbutt was on a three-year contract, at £20,000 a year, and after his first season Keith came to me and said that he'd promised Mabbutt that if he made a good start to his Spurs career he would tear up the agreement and give him a better one. "What do you want to give him?" I asked Keith. "£50,000 a year," he replied. I thought that was a crazy increase, and suggested £35,000. Keith was not happy about that, so as a compromise, we agreed that it would be £40,000. A couple of months later, I was discussing a new contract offer for another Spurs player with Peter Day [Tottenham's secretary] and he just happened to say: "Well, Gary Mabbutt is on £50,000 . . ." I couldn't believe it but, on seeing the contract, I had to.'

Scholar's perceived interference into what Burkinshaw considered to be his own territory continued to gnaw away at the manager, who became so sensitive about the demarcation lines between Scholar and himself that he virtually started retaliating before his space had even been invaded. The final straw for him came in 1984, before Tottenham's second-leg UEFA Cup quarter-final away to Austria Vienna. 'Scholar, Paul Bobroff [the head of Tottenham's holding company] and I met in a hotel bedroom on the afternoon of the game, and we had a big row,' Burkinshaw recalls. 'The pair of them wanted me to let them have the power, and I was not going to give in to them. I went into that match seething.'

Once again, Scholar's version of events differs. 'It was merely suggested that the secretary and myself deal with players' contracts, under his supervision.' At any rate, Tottenham got through to the semi-final and Burkinshaw, who announced that he would be resigning from White Hart Lane at the end of the season, went on to give his chairman and the club the most dramatic of parting gifts – victory over Anderlecht, on penalties, in the UEFA Cup final.

Today, Burkinshaw, now aged 62 and living in Hertfordshire, also remembers his other parting shot – his famous remark: 'There used to be a football club here.' Referring to Scholar's ill-fated move in turning Tottenham into a multi-faceted public limited company, he says: 'The point I was trying to get across was that Irving Scholar had come in and turned the place into a commercial enterprise. Nothing wrong in that, but when it started happening, it concerned me that football would be forgotten about and, as far as I was concerned, that's what happened. He said that the game had got too big for managers like me to have the control we used to have, but you see what happened after I left. They threw money about all over the place, things went wrong and the club went down the pan.'

Scholar, too, has a long memory. He remembers in particular that when he took over the club, they carried the burden of the biggest debt – £5.5 million – in the league. While it is difficult to dispute totally Burkinshaw's suggestion that Scholar made too many mistakes, you could argue that the chairman's errors stemmed mainly from the fact that his ideas were too far ahead of their time and that at least they came from a genuine affection for Spurs and the game.

Scholar's affection for Tottenham was not inherited from his father, a gent's hairdresser who worked six days a week and took no interest in football, but from his mother's brother, who took the young Scholar to his first Tottenham match, against Cardiff City in 1952, when he was barely six. From that moment, Scholar says, he was 'hooked'. Later, he also became hooked on making a success of his life. Educated at Marylebone Grammar School in central London, Scholar, whose first job at 16 was in an estate agent's office for £6 a week, made his fortune as a property developer. His big break, he recalls, came in 1973 when he joined forces with a friend to form a joint company with European Ferries to develop office buildings in London and the south-east of England. It confirmed his belief in the work ethic and strengthened his equally valuable asset of being sharp enough to take advantage of every opportunity.

He insists that it was never his intention to become chairman of Tottenham or any other club, arguing that the initial motivation for his desire to establish himself as more than just another well-heeled Spurs supporter was to force Tottenham to listen to him and accept his help.

Scholar, who watched Tottenham each Saturday – home and away – with his friends, had become disenchanted with the club's apparent meanness in the transfer market and lack of dynamic leadership. But what really disturbed him was the news in 1981 concerning the rebuilding of the old West Stand, which the club estimated would cost £3.5 million. Scholar, involved at the time in commercial rebuilding projects, was convinced that the club had miscalculated, and that this mistake could have a disastrous effect on the field. He wasn't the only one who thought this way.

Earlier, Sid Wale, Tottenham's chairman since 1969 and the largest single shareholder in the club with a holding of around 14 per cent (compared with the other directors' 5 per cent), had been reluctant to authorise the project. He paid a heavy price for his stubbornness by becoming the target of a boardroom coup which saw him forced to resign in the face of a no-confidence vote in him; he was replaced by Richardson.

Annoyed by Richardson's arrogant attitude towards him when he offered advice, Scholar put up more of a fight — to put it mildly. Indeed, as football club take-over battles go, White Hart Lane has gone down as a classic. In most cases, clubs change owners only when they are in financial trouble, a situation in which anyone coming forward with the money to buy the controlling interest, and take responsibility for the club's debts, is likely to be welcomed with open arms. You don't have to pay the earth for a club either, at least not initially. Ken Bates paid the nominal sum of just £1 for control of Chelsea, as did Barry Hearn when he came to Leyton Orient's rescue. But the Scholar scenario was different. Tottenham did not seem to be in serious financial difficulties when he started asking awkward questions about the finances of the club at their AGM in September 1981; in any case Richardson and his directors looked upon themselves as being in a closed shop. But Scholar's doggedness was remarkable. The idea of forcing his way into that shop, he recalls, came to him while he was driving to a Tottenham match at Leeds shortly after the AGM. It was to become an obsession.

The rest of that year was spent wading through the list of Tottenham shareholders. He found a high number of them were women, and working on the assumption that they had inherited their shares from their husbands or fathers, and had no interest in football themselves, he decided to write offering £250 a share to anyone owning between one and 20, £150 a share for those holding between 20 and 50, and £100 to those with more. It was a painstaking process. Only 4,892 Tottenham shares were in issue, and these were in the hands of between 500 and 600 people, of whom 360 held only one share each.

This, though, was the least of his problems. The major stumbling block was Article 14 in the club's Articles of Association, which gave directors the right to bar the registration of shares to anybody they did not approve of. The Articles had already been challenged legally, by a Hubert Berry way back in 1935, but the court had ruled in the directors' favour. The high-powered legal advisers Scholar employed confirmed that the precedent of that case in English law meant he had little chance of faring any better. But his barrister also told him: 'Whilst the directors have the power to stop anyone being recognised as a new shareholder, they can't prevent a sale taking place.' He advised Scholar to get his solicitor to formulate a Deed of Trust, effectively giving him legal ownership and getting those who had sold shares to him to give an undertaking to name him as their proxy and always carry out his wishes on any matters relating to the shares. As Scholar later wrote in his book: 'I knew I had found the secret key to unlock the stubborn Spurs board. Even at this stage, I had no thought of a takeover. What I was attempting to do was to buy enough shares to bring a little influence to bear. Perhaps at the very best, I might get a seat on the board.'

By this time, Scholar had left England to live in Monaco, but with a friend helping him he managed to trace Hubert Berry's widow, Elsie – the third-biggest shareholder with 297 – and buy her holding. 'I became the company's largest single shareholder, with more than 800 shares, overtaking Sidney Wale who had 734,' he recalls. Then came the biggest breakthrough of all. Still inevitably nursing some resentment towards the régime which had forced him out of office, Wale contacted Scholar to offer him his shares, too. Scholar bought all but 34 of Wale's stock, to give himself 35 per cent. Scholar had bought his beloved Spurs. He was in control.

Even then, he was happy to take a back seat, and not flex his muscles publicly for another 12 or 15 months. It appealed to his sense of fun that Article 14, while not having had the desired effect of keeping him out, was preventing Richardson from knowing his plans.

As it turned out, Scholar revealed his hand earlier than he intended, as a result of a newspaper report of a speech by Tottenham's club physician, Dr Brian Curtin, drawing attention to the threat of Tottenham's boardroom régime being ousted by Scholar (whom he did not name), and the sorry financial plight of the club. Scholar's reaction was to come forward with two offers, both of which were dependent on Richardson resigning and Douglas Alexiou (Wale's son-in-law) taking his place. One part of the offer was a £700,000 interest-free loan, the second part a pledge to underwrite a new £600,000 shares issue.

Richardson put up the barricades, but in the meantime Scholar was given another boost when Paul Bobroff (then known to Scholar only as a Tottenham executive-box owner and the head of a property company which had been successfully floated on the Stock Exchange) contacted him to reveal that he had become Tottenham's second-biggest shareholder. Bobroff, who had bought his 13 per cent block from an estate previously determined to hold on to it, offered to sell the shares to Scholar at the same price he had paid for them, in return for a seat on Scholar's proposed new board.

Scholar declined the offer, opting instead to go into partnership with Bobroff. In hindsight, he feels this was one of his biggest mistakes, on the grounds that Bobroff was more of a Tottenham Hotspur businessman than a Tottenham Hotspur fan and did not have Scholar's 'feel' for the soccer side of the club. Initially, however, the tie-up between Scholar and Bobroff put the pair in the unassailable position of owning 50 per cent of the club's shares, and sounded the death knell for the men they were striving to oust.

On 1 December 1983, Scholar called an EGM demanding the resignations of Richardson, his son Geoffrey, and Ken Kennard, their major boardroom supporter. The trio did not wait for the official vote of no confidence – they resigned the following day.

To Scholar, inevitably remote from the day-to-day running of the club because of his business responsibilities in the South of France, it was perfectly logical to leave himself off the new board and to make Alexiou, a man whom he could trust not to undermine or destroy the club's football image, the chairman. It made perfect sense to him, too, to float the club on the Stock Exchange, a move which meant the formation of a holding company for the football club; Bobroff, more experienced than Scholar when it came to high finance City matters, was put in charge of it.

The £3.8 million raised by the flotation in October 1983, together with a new £1.1 million share issue underwritten by Scholar and Bobroff, cleared up Tottenham's debts. But, for Scholar, there was a clear warning sign of what could lie ahead. As he wrote in his book: 'The financial advisers [on Tottenham's move to become a public limited company] had insisted that in order to attract investors, the offer document should state that Tottenham would become "a broadly based leisure company". I could see future problems in such a commitment, but Bobroff made it clear that if the company wanted to take advantage of the money on offer, certain concessions had to be made. The City, he said, were not handing us £3.8 million without expecting any sort of return. What they wanted us to do was diversify and make larger profits, to enable them to have larger dividend cheques.'

Though Scholar concedes that the concept was sound in principle, he claims that Tottenham plc, headed by Bobroff, fell into the diversification trap of entering potential income fields which were either too far removed from football or not subject to strict enough control and guidance. To Tottenham Football Club – at which Scholar at last became chairman in the summer of 1984 – were added companies dealing in sports clothing, women's fashions and computerised ticketing systems. The latter, Synchro Systems, proved a particularly costly mistake. The company was making profits of around £100,000 a year when Tottenham bought it for £120,000, but it eventually ran into financial trouble to the tune of £1.5 million and was offloaded for just £1.

Such problems for Tottenham plc had a considerable knock-on effect concerning Scholar's ambitions to revive the playing side's glory days. In that respect, the nightmare for him truly started shortly after the 1990 World Cup finals in Italy when Spurs, who had fallen £10.5 million into debt, were involved in a desperate struggle to find the balance of the £1.5 million transfer fee – some £900,000 – that was due to be paid to Barcelona for Gary Lineker and Nayim by the start of August. Scholar cleared that barrier by obtaining a £1.1 million loan from Robert Maxwell, an arrangement which meant his having to put up the assets of his property company as a guarantee. But with Maxwell (then Derby's owner) changing his mind about buying a stake in the club, and wiping out that massive bank overdraft by underwriting a new £12 million share issue, things went from bad to worse.

The prospect of Spurs having to return Lineker to Barcelona had been disturbing enough for Scholar. But, with the bank putting increasing pressure on Tottenham plc to reduce their overdraft from £10.5 million to £2.5 million, he faced an even more agonising situation with Paul Gascoigne – one of his three all-time favourite Spurs stars alongside Alan Gilzean and Chris Waddle. As a result of his World Cup performances in Italy, Gascoigne, bought from Newcastle for £2 million in 1988, was now worth around four times that in the transfer market. But while Scholar's plc colleagues talked with ever more strident voices about the advantages of selling him – indeed, of the need to do so to get Tottenham out of their financial mess – Scholar donned his Spurs supporter's hat and dug his heels in.

Eventually, early in the 1990–91 season, Scholar was persuaded to at least go through the motions of eliciting bids for Gascoigne, if only to show the bank that Tottenham were taking action to improve their financial situation. However, Lazio, bidding £7 million for Gascoigne, quickly created a transfer momentum that even Scholar found difficult to stop. Determined not to give in to Spurs' holding company, he had tried all manner of delaying tactics, including that of appointing an agent who had fallen out with Gascoigne's business manager to handle the sale on Tottenham's behalf. Gascoigne himself unwittingly gave him a helping hand by suddenly demanding a £1 million cut from the transfer fee. At this stage, the player, inevitably dazzled by the riches being dangled in front of him by the Italian club, had become conditioned to thinking that his days at White Hart Lane were numbered. Thus, when the possibility of Tottenham finding a backer *à la* Maxwell did not materialise, and having failed to tie the knot in negotiations for his shareholding with a consortium involving Spurs manager Terry Venables and the boxing promoter Frank Warren, Scholar was forced to face the inevitable.

The Tottenham soap opera then took two dramatic twists. Scholar's beloved Gascoigne, whose tears in the World Cup in Italy had endeared him to millions, cried again after just 19 minutes of Tottenham's 2–1 FA Cup final victory over Nottingham Forest, through the knee injury which was to put him out of action for more than a year. Tottenham, with Venables and Alan Sugar having bought Scholar's shares and shown him the White Hart Lane exit door, let the player go to Lazio at the reduced fee of £5.4 million.

Having had the opportunity to sell out to Maxwell, Scholar elected to press ahead in the direction of Alan Sugar and Terry Venables because of the newspaper tycoon's notorious unpredictability and perversity. But, referring to the nuts and bolts of the Sugar-Venables rescue act in his book, Scholar wrote: 'For me, the crucial question in all this was whether the club would be secure and whether we could somehow still hold on to Paul Gascoigne.' He claims he was then astonished to learn from Nat Solomon (Bobroff's successor as the Tottenham plc chairman) that the offer of Venables and Sugar was conditional on the sale of Gascoigne for not less than £4.5 million. 'After I had recovered from my shock, I started laughing,' Scholar said. 'For months there had been any number of stories in the press as to how keen Terry was to keep Gascoigne at White Hart Lane; how, if he was allowed to take over the club, he would do everything in his power to make sure [the player would stay]. I was painted as the villain of the piece, the man who said he wanted to keep Gascoigne but was secretly planning to sell him.'

That allegation, made by a newspaper, led to Scholar winning £100,000 in libel damages. Nonetheless, the view among a number of Tottenham fans that he has much to answer for (an opinion which was heightened in 1994 when Tottenham were revealed to have made irregular payments to players during the Scholar-Venables régime and were clobbered by the FA as a consequence) still bothers him.

'It's painful in a sense, because you'd like people to think that you tried your best and did everything for the right reasons,' he says. 'The reality of the situation was that the company I was chairman of had to foot the bill for problems elsewhere. Unfortunately, the press just see headlines and that's it. Nobody scrapes the surface, which is one of the reasons why I wrote my book. But people still harp on about the so-called mess I left the club in and how Sugar and Venables saved it. I've had to bear the brunt of it ever since. I've had to carry the guilt and everything else.'

What hurts him more than anything is the view that he almost caused Tottenham to be declared bankrupt. He has always maintained that despite the warning noises emanating from Tottenham's bankers, the club's position at the time he left − their debts had risen to £11 million − was not as critical as it might have seemed. In addition to the sale of Gascoigne, they were also poised to get a £5.5 million cash injection through season-ticket sales and executive-box agreements. 'Let me tell you something − under no circumstances would Tottenham have folded,' Scholar insists. 'We had £20 million worth of players, £20 million worth of ground − where was the problem? Thousands of companies would have liked to have been in that situation, and so would their bankers. On top of all this, we had won the FA Cup the previous season and, in addition to the potential income from the European Cup-Winners Cup, we had negotiated an exclusive £700,000 deal with ITV for the screening of our home ties. In any event, we could have sold Gascoigne much earlier than we did, and if I had just been interested in myself, we would have done so. Sell Gascoigne for £7 million, financial problems zero. But to me, that was letting the team down, it was letting the supporters down. That was my thinking.

'We were coming out of the woods when we won the FA Cup,

and what I should have done was sit tight and stick it out until the financial situation had been completely sorted. But things were being made extremely difficult for me by the media. There were headlines virtually every day; the adverse publicity I got was relentless. It was like a nightmare.' All of this left Scholar feeling some resentment towards Terry Venables, who he suggests exploited his stature and his media contacts to wage a propaganda war against him.

In some ways, the picture Scholar paints of his relationship with Venables is similar to the one that Sugar has constructed, following his controversial sacking of Venables. As with the association between the latter couple, the link between Scholar and Venables seemed ideal when it started in November 1987. Venables, having made a big international name for himself as Barcelona's coach, was the fourth manager to work under Scholar (apart from Burkinshaw, the others were Peter Shreeves and David Pleat); and had a far higher media profile than the others.

He was also the most ambitious of the quartet, particularly with regards to developing his interests in areas outside that of merely football management. One of the most common criticisms levelled at Venables is that he has taken his quest to broaden his personal horizons too much to the extreme; that he would have been much better off concentrating on his expertise as a football coach. Scholar, who once described his manager as having a 'grasshopper' mind, admits that this did not bother him at the time he appointed Venables. One person to whom he turned for advice told him: 'Appointing Venables is probably the right decision now, but you will regret it.'

'We actually had a very good relationship at one time. I have to say that,' Scholar says. 'I was working very hard to try and deliver what he wanted, which was plenty of money to spend in the transfer market. Some of his purchases were disappointing – I think he acknowledged that himself – but I always tried to support him.'

So when did it go wrong? 'I think it was possibly when I was negotiating with him over a new contract. I was a bit concerned that he was involved in all sorts of different things outside Tottenham, so I thought it would make sense to put him on a slightly lower salary but with large bonuses. He got the needle with that. He thought I was trying to short-change him. But, in fairness, he hadn't delivered yet – he'd been with Tottenham for three or four years and we hadn't won anything, not even come close. So I said to him: "Fine, tell me what you want and I'll try and get the board to agree." But not once did he commit himself on this or give a figure.'

Scholar, sensitive about reopening too many old sores, is reticent when expanding on his relationship with Venables. He has kept an even lower public profile on the debate concerning Venables's somewhat stormier relationship with Sugar.

Initially, the two men bought their way in to Spurs as partners, with Venables finding the £3 million necessary for this through loans from his company, Eddenote. But before long, Sugar was struck with the feeling that Venables, who was installed as Tottenham's chief executive in the aftermath of the pair's takeover, with the day-to-day running of the team handed to Shreeves and then Doug Livermore and Ray Clemence, was becoming too big for his boots. To Sugar, Venables was no more than a football pro whose determination to impose himself on other aspects of the club and, indeed, run the club from top to bottom, outweighed his capabilities. And when Tottenham had a rights issue in December 1991, Sugar put himself in a strong position to do something about it by increasing his shareholding to 50 per cent and leaving Venables as a minority shareholder with 23 per cent.

In essence, their clash was little different to the one that had occurred between Scholar and Burkinshaw. But in the case of Sugar and Venables, it created an explosion which reverberated around the game long after Venables' acrimonious departure from White Hart Lane in 1993. The feud between the two men continued even when Terry became England coach, a position which highlighted such sideshows as Venables suing Sugar for wrongful dismissal and Sugar banning him from watching Tottenham home matches.

Those close to Scholar claim that he anticipated such problems from the start. When Sugar and Venables took control of the club, a friend asked him: 'What do you think is going to happen?' Scholar replied: 'The first year will be the honeymoon, the second year will be the divorce.' Scholar himself would have been happy to pass on his thoughts on the matter to Sugar, except that a meeting arranged between the two men was cancelled by the former on the grounds that his insistence on strict secrecy was not adhered to.

The two did finally meet two years later, shortly after Venables was sacked. After listening to Sugar complaining about Venables, Scholar told him: 'You have found out what I was going to tell you two years ago.' Sugar told him that he made up his mind to part company with Venables when he was walking out of Wembley Stadium following Tottenham's 1–0 FA Cup semi-final defeat by Arsenal in April 1993. 'What would you have done had Tottenham won that match and gone on to win the Cup?' Scholar asked. 'I would have needed big balls to have done it then, wouldn't I?' Sugar retorted, giving the faint impression that he would have relished the challenge.

Sugar, indeed, is a man who shoots from the hip, and Venables has not been his only target.

THREE

Young Guns

Arsenal's Eton-educated Peter Hill-Wood, a director of
Hambros Bank, stands out as being the most 'blue-blooded' of
the Premiership chairmen. He is nothing if not a traditionalist. So
when you visit the 60-year-old Hill-Wood at his Chelsea apartment,
the obvious question to put to him is what does he feel about some
of the 'new money' entrepreneurs in charge of clubs nowadays –
and, more specifically, his tough soccer neighbour at White Hart
Lane?

'I have found Alan Sugar to be one of the least charming people
I've ever come across,' said Hill-Wood in his impeccable cut-glass
accent. 'He may be perfectly reasonable, but I have never felt comfortable having a conversation with him.' Do they bump into each
other socially? 'No,' he replied, keeping a straight face. 'I wouldn't
particularly want to.'

It is rare that Hill-Wood, whose upper-class family have directed
Arsenal's affairs from the boardroom for almost 70 years – for the
most part with an unrivalled sense of political and social correctness
– is as outspoken as this. He is a humorous, erudite man, the sort
of figure you might expect to see in the MCC committee-room or
in the secretary's chair at an exclusive golf club. But as Arsenal see

themselves as English football's royal family, the recent blow to their image has made it increasingly difficult for him to avoid retaliation. At the time I met Hill-Wood, for example, Arsenal had been under heavy fire from the media – and especially from *The Sun* – when the club had been very much in Sugar's gun-sights.

At the start of the 1995–96 season, Sugar reportedly described Arsenal as 'gutless' and having 'no balls' over the fact that, instead of sacking their manager George Graham immediately they learned he had pocketed £425,000 of the money the club paid for the transfers of John Jensen and Paul Lyderson, they waited for the Premiership commission's inquiry into the matter to be completed some months later before parting company with him. As if not satisfied he had damaged Arsenal enough, at a time when they were also striving to eradicate the embarrassment created by the ill-discipline of some of their star players, Sugar also accused the Gunners of setting a potentially destructive inflationary example in transfer wages and players' salaries. Though some viewed this as a case of the pot calling the kettle black – it was believed that Tottenham had broken their own wage structure the previous season in buying Jürgen Klinsmann, Ilie Dumitrescu and Gheorghe Popescu – he described Arsenal's expenditure on Dennis Bergkamp as 'irresponsible'. He added: 'Arsenal have taken an almighty risk. There is no way he is going to have the same effect as Klinsmann. As the season progresses, and the fog, ice and cold arrive, his approach could change, especially when someone gives him a good kicking, an elbow in the ribs or a whack on the earhole.' As for Arsenal's claim that they were interested in signing more foreign stars, Sugar said: 'They are good talkers, that lot, aren't they?'

All good fun; but not to Hill-Wood. For once, his sensitivity about Arsenal's old image as the 'aristocracy' of English football made it impossible for him to avoid the temptation of a response. 'He [Sugar] did write me a letter about all this,' he said. 'I think it was meant to be an apology, although if you read it carefully, it didn't actually apologise for anything. He denied it, and said he'd been quoted out of context and all this. But I don't know – I mean, he doesn't like verbal abuse so he shouldn't go hurling it at other people.'

Sugar (who might have been tempted to be more diplomatic when his daughter started dating the son of Arsenal vice-chairman David Dein) did have a point about Arsenal's handling of the Graham affair. But then the Spurs man, on top of the differences between his background and Hill-Wood's, is not as deeply entrenched in the traditions of the game, and especially in those of a club like Arsenal.

When the Arsenal board met to discuss a successor to Don Howe in 1986, and failed to land Terry Venables from Barcelona, George Graham had been Hill-Wood's choice for the job ahead of Alex Ferguson, who was then at Aberdeen. David Dein, the most assertive of the Arsenal directors, on the other hand, felt that the positions of the two contenders should be the other way around. Hill-Wood had good cause to feel vindicated. Graham became the most successful manager in Arsenal's history, bringing five trophies to the club – including two Championships and the European Cup-Winners Cup – in eight years. He also seemed very much the Arsenal 'type'; loyal to the cause, respectable, thrifty and capable of setting the highest standards in terms of the professionalism of his teams. So it was perhaps typical of Hill-Wood's mentality that he should want to give Graham the benefit of the doubt for as long as possible – that he should believe Arsenal owed Graham a 'duty of care' for what he had done for the club. One Arsenal insider reveals that 'Hill-Wood was shocked by the Graham revelations, but at the same time, you get the impression that he felt sorry for him. You know: "Oh, the poor chap – how can we sack him when he's got the Inland Revenue on his back, and problems like that?"'

Sugar would have taken a less liberal stance. But old habits die hard, and Alex Fynn, the author of *Heroes and Villains*, a book on the rivalry between Tottenham and Arsenal, points out that: 'For years, Arsenal had been run as a benevolent autocracy. Those in control, who had come from public-school backgrounds, liked football and they believed in doing things the "right" way.'

Terry Neill, the former Arsenal player and manager, had as much experience of this as anyone. 'There was a sense of permanency about the place, an established order and a sense that everything had to be in its proper place,' he said. 'I remember on one occasion Alan Ball [one of Arsenal's key players] being sent off a week before an important FA Cup tie. Under the FA rules then, he could have been available for the tie if we had appealed, but Hill-Wood would not allow us to do so because he didn't think it was the right thing to do.' Neill also recalled that, when he became manager, he mentioned to Hill-Wood that if the club ever wanted to get rid of him, he would prefer the deed to be done before Christmas, so he could have the rare treat of being able to spend the festive period with his family. Neill was sacked on 16 December 1983.

Graham was the last of the all-powerful football managers in England; or rather Arsenal, with their comparatively old-fashioned Establishment hierarchy, were the last big club at which someone like him could fully flex his muscles.

In that context, Hill-Wood gave an interesting insight into his working relationship with Graham in a book published in 1990 to commemorate Arsenal's 1989 Championship triumph. 'I never get involved in the day-to-day running of the club,' Hill-Wood wrote. 'It has never been any different at Arsenal. We have a managing director in Ken Friar who looks after the business side of the operation, and a manager, George Graham, who looks after the playing side. If George wanted to spend a million pounds on a player, it would not need a board meeting before he could go ahead. That may sound rather casual but it is the way we do things. He decides the level of the fee it would be reasonable to pay. He usually discusses it with Ken Friar. One of them, probably George, would telephone and say what he wanted to do. I would have a brief conversation with him, basically asking all the obvious questions and would then ask George to get Ken Friar to telephone all the other directors and tell them what we are proposing to do. We have never yet had a case where one of the directors has said: "This is sheer lunacy, we must meet to discuss it."' Hill-Wood described Graham as a man 'sensible enough to know, without any guidelines, where to draw the line', and added: 'Up to now, I have granted every request made by George Graham.'

All of which made the Graham transfer-market 'bungs' scandal doubly hard to take for his chairman. In the aftermath of it, he shook his head sadly and told me: 'I think it has come home to us pretty starkly that our manager had far too much latitude. Not only this, I did not realise, and I don't think any other member of the board realised, that his job specification had actually become too big for him, too big for any one man. There are a lot of people at Arsenal, and the manager has to realise that it is important to delegate.'

In truth, despite his boardroom position at Highbury, Hill-Wood represents something of a soft target for Arsenal critics. The Arsenal chairman he might be, but that does not mean he can run the show or even exert the biggest influence on the club. The same can be said about his counterparts at Blackburn and Wimbledon, who are owned respectively by Jack Walker and Sam Hammam, but whose chairmen are Robert Coar and Stanley Reed. In Arsenal's case, although they have had one of the most democratic boards in the Premiership, in terms of the extent to which the shares have been spread among their directors, it is Dein who is recognised as the strongest force behind the club's policies.

When I interviewed Hill-Wood, the last available Arsenal annual report showed that, of the 70,000 ordinary shares owned by the seven directors, he had the second smallest number – 448 – behind Ken Friar. Dein was among those with the most. Hill-Wood says: 'There are three major shareholders on the Arsenal board, and I don't know whether any of them would want one of the others to be chairman. They could get rid of me tomorrow if they wanted to, but the advantages of having me in the chair is that I am neutral; I can be a little more objective and independent.

'We are all different,' he adds. 'We do have our arguments – I think it would be unhealthy if we didn't – and I don't agree with all the things that are pushed through. But I assume the other directors are happy with the way it works.'

At one time, Dein had 42 per cent of the shares, three times as many as the rest of the board put together but, according to reports, had been forced to reduce his stake and 'sacrifice' his controlling interest when his business ran into financial difficulties. A report in the *Mail on Sunday* in January 1995 said that Dein had sold a number of his shares to his close friend Danny Fiszman, a diamond and property dealer who had come onto the board as a result, and that the two men had a joint interest in a smaller block. But Dein remained the largest single shareholder and, with Fiszman's support, had lost little of his voting power.

Dein has become one of the most influential figures in English football, let alone Arsenal – not bad going for someone who, little more than a decade ago, was just another well-heeled season-ticket-holder. In some ways, Dein's entry into the inner sanctum of the professional game, at its policy-shaping boardroom level, has recently been mirrored on the other side of London by the emergence of Matthew Harding as a key member of the hierarchy of Chelsea. However, one of the differences between the rise of the two men into the position of vice-chairman is that Harding's has been achieved against a background of much acrimony and controversy.

The 42-year-old Harding, chairman of the Benfield Insurance Group and holder of a personal fortune of some £150 million, had been devoted to Chelsea since he was a young boy. Like Dein, he delighted in mingling socially with his team's players; and, like Dein, he badly wanted to be part of the club. That dream – realised with a place on the board in 1992 – cost him more than £25 million. Through the club's holding company, Chelsea Village, he bought the freehold of Stamford Bridge, thus becoming the club's landlord; he provided much of the cash for the rebuilding of their north stand; and he endeared himself to manager Glenn Hoddle, not to mention the fans, by financing transfer deals.

To those who spent a lot of time in his company, it was clear that Harding felt Bates was concentrating too much on developing the Stamford Bridge site into a glorious leisure and shopping complex instead of spending the money he and Hoddle deemed necessary to end the team's image as perennial under-achievers. He even talked of buying out Bates and taking control himself.

Unfortunately for Harding, he did not pick the easiest of adversaries. The notoriously aggressive Bates has a street-fighter's mentality – as one of his friends said: 'If Ken hasn't got a fight on his hands, he'll go out looking for one. He does love a battle.' Dein himself can testify to this after crossing swords with 'Blaster Bates' on issues such as TV contracts and the number of matches a top club should play. Certainly, as one of the longest-serving chairmen in Britain, Bates knows all there is to know about boardroom politics.

The battle between him and Harding began in earnest in 1995 when Harding resigned as a director of Chelsea Village over the fact that 66 per cent of the company was owned by nominee companies based in Guernsey; it was understood that he did not feel comfortable about involving himself in a company in which the identity of the majority shareholders was not known. In November 1995, Bates, never one to bother about adverse publicity, responded to the pressure that Harding was putting on him by banning Harding from the Chelsea directors' box and even withdrawing his director's car-parking ticket. In a letter to Harding, Bates accused him of waging a campaign against him – of 'pretending to be a good friend of mine, working together amicably, while rubbishing me and Suzanne [Bates's girlfriend] at every opportunity behind my back during the course of courting certain parts of the press'.

The situation became increasingly farcical, and damaging to Chelsea's image, with the two men scoring points off one another in the tabloids. After one match against Tottenham, which Bates missed because of illness, Harding was smuggled into Hoddle's office by the manager via the Stamford Bridge laundry room and a fire escape.

Eventually, a sort of ceasefire was declared, and Harding got his director's privileges back. Bates, however, continued as chairman – as firmly in the Stamford Bridge driving seat as ever. Moreover, having taken a decisive lead in his battle against Harding, Bates achieved a more significant victory in May 1996.

Harding had been negotiating with Bates to convert his investment in Chelsea into shares. That would have meant his gaining a 25.1 per cent stake in Chelsea Village; becoming vice-chairman of the company; and, perhaps even more attractive to him, becoming head of a committee overseeing the football side of the club. However, the talks between the two men broke down when Harding's lawyers imposed fresh conditions which they insisted were not negotiable; and as journalist Mihir Bose reported in the *Daily Telegraph*: 'Harding now finds himself a somewhat less substantial shareholder in the company. According to the conditions of one of the loans Harding had given Chelsea [£5 million], the loan could be converted into shares. This is now giving Harding an 11 per cent stake in the company. It is a position that gives him little clout, however, since Bates not only owns 28 per cent but has the proxy for the remainder, owned by the offshore nominee companies.'

The two men seem to have resolved their differences since then. But the episode must have been a blow to Harding's pride. One observer, a former chairman, felt that Bates had 'played Harding like a violin'.

Cynics might argue that David Dein has done likewise with Peter Hill-Wood to get into the position of power he now occupies at Highbury. Hill-Wood does not see it that way, and nor does Dein. However, while it would be stretching a point to say that Dein outsmarted Hill-Wood, the latter does agree that Dein was helped by the chairman's lack of foresight on how English football could be developed. Hill-Wood, bound by the football traditions with which he had been brought up, and more specifically by the 'values' of Arsenal, did not altogether appreciate the game's commercial potential and found it difficult to visualise the ways in which clubs might capitalise on it. As he admits: 'Because of my upbringing and background and whatever, I have never looked at a football club as a financial asset. In the old days, when any shares came up for sale, we used to draw lots for them at the board meetings. We used to buy them at thirty bob each, and if you got them, you were inclined to think that they were a waste of money. One didn't view it in a commercial way.'

But Dein, while unquestionably having the best interests of Arsenal at heart, was more aware of their potential. Referring to Dein's determination in acquiring Arsenal shares, Hill-Wood recalled: 'David had a go at me – well, I say "had a go", but he initially wanted to get involved some time before he actually did, and he just kept going at it. He is extremely persistent.'

Dein's entry into the Arsenal boardroom came in 1983 as a result of his persuading Arsenal to sell him more than 1,000 unissued shares for £330,000, thus giving him a 14 per cent stake in the club.

Hill-Wood winced when reminded that, at the time, he described Dein's offer as 'dead money'. His actual words, which have haunted him ever since, were: 'Some men like to buy fast cars or racehorses or yachts, but David is more interested in Arsenal. I am delighted, but I still think he is crazy. To all intents and purposes, it is dead money.' No doubt, Hill-Wood took the same view a couple of years later, when Arsenal's quest to raise the money to rebuild their north stand led to a 7 for 1 share issue; and Hill-Wood selling Dein another block from his own increased total.

Irving Scholar, who likes to think that he blazed a trail for Dein to follow with his similarly bold, dramatic inroads into the Tottenham boardroom in 1982, suggests that Hill-Wood should not feel too badly about any of this. 'Remember you are talking about [events that happened] 13 years ago. What would the £300,000 David put in initially be worth today? £1.5 million? £2 million? Right, imagine someone turning up on the doorstep of a Premiership club and saying: "I am a lifelong supporter prepared to put in £2 million for a small stake in the company." Who's going to say no?'

What are the shares Hill-Wood sold worth now? 'Don't ask me,' the Arsenal chairman says. 'A lot more – maybe ten times what I sold them for. I thought he was paying a silly price, but he has done incredibly well and I've done very badly, so clearly he was right.' He pauses, and shakes his head again in wonderment at Dein's persistence. 'He is like a dog with a bone once he gets an idea into his head, even when his ideas are wrong. You know, if he's told "No, we're not going to do that", he doesn't ever take no for an answer. Two months later, he'll come up with it again. "For Christ's sake, David, we told you we are not going to do it – it doesn't make sense," we'll tell him. "Well, I've thought of doing it in another way," he'll say.' Hill-Wood smiles. 'I don't mind that, I think it's good.'

Those who know Dein single out 'ambitiousness' and 'persistence' as being two of his major characteristics. He himself likes to portray himself as a man of action. Hill-Wood is not the only person who can testify to this. Rick Parry, the Premiership's chief executive, marvels at Dein's energy: 'David can be on the phone at any time. He can be on the phone to me at eight in the morning, for no other reason than he is driving somewhere and wants to use the time to do something productive. "Any great things happening?" he'll ask. I say: "If they did, David, they happened while I was asleep in bed."'

The PFA's Gordon Taylor adds: 'He's like a racehorse that you sometimes want to put reins and blinkers on.'

Both Parry and Taylor delivered the comments as a compliment rather than a criticism. As for other views about Dein, it is not so easy to tell in the cases of his old adversaries, Ken Bates and Ron Noades. On the subject of how Dein and Philip Carter helped push the clubs into that television deal with BSB in 1988, Noades, referring to the pair's enforced departure from the League Management Committee as a consequence, admits that he would have preferred Dein to go and Carter to stay. 'I happened to think that Carter was the best president the league had and, in fact, I said to David that if he [Dein] stood down from the committee, I reckoned Carter could survive. But according to David, he and Carter had agreed to stand or fall together. It was a pity . . .' Noades shrugged, and added: 'Look, I don't want to give the impression that I don't like or respect David – it's not the case. David and I are good friends, actually. But in my opinion, he is inclined to do things for the good of Arsenal, whereas Ken [Bates] and I try to put the emphasis on doing things for the good of football.'

Where this impression of Dein does not altogether hold up, of course, is that in addition to his position at Highbury, he is a member of the FA Council, the FA's International Committee and the FA's Finance Committee. Some might have mixed feelings about the image he can present ('He reminds me a bit of the Michael Douglas character in the film *Wall Street*,' says one observer) but as Dein points out, 'If people didn't think I had the ability, or something to contribute, I wouldn't be voted on to these committees.'

There can be little doubt that his impact at Highbury has been impressive by any standards. Through his expertise in the development of Arsenal stadium and their commercial set-up, Dein has played as big a part in boosting the Gunners' income as any of their team managers and players.

Hill-Wood pointed out that when Arsenal paid what was then a club record £80,000 transfer fee for Frank McLintock in 1964, their turnover was £250,000, virtually all of which came through gate receipts. It was still the same story in 1983, when the turnover was £2 million, and even by 1988, the year that Dein gave up his business in favour of becoming Arsenal's chief executive. But by 1995 Arsenal's income was £25 million – and the Dein-led commercial and marketing set-up was contributing no less than half of it.

For many years, though, Dein might have been struggling to get anywhere near the boardroom of a club like Arsenal – a point that Hill-Wood does not dispute.

Arsenal was a club which epitomised the family dynasty syndrome, with shares treated like gold-dust by those who inherited them, if only from a prestige point of view. 'One sort of stepped into grandfathers' and fathers' shoes – one did not buy one's way in, having suddenly made a great fortune,' Hill-Wood said. The shoes have been of the highest quality, as one would expect of a club long regarded as the classiest in Britain. The present directors include Sir Robert Bellinger, the former Lord Mayor of London and the oldest of the group at 85; Sir Roger Gibbs, the chairman of Wellcome Trust medical charity organisation; and the Carr brothers, Clive (a Park Lane hotelier) and Richard (a barrister) who have together held in trust the 29,000 shares of their uncle, Sir Guy Bracewell-Smith.

The latter was Arsenal's chairman between the reigns of Hill-Wood's grandfather, Sir Samuel, and his father, Dennis. The former, who founded the club, was on the Arsenal board from 1919 until 1952, the latter from 1952 until 1982. It was in 1982 that Hill-Wood, having been a director for 21 years, took on the chairman's role himself: 'I had no doubts about doing it,' he recalls. 'Anyway, at the time, I think I was the only director who wanted to do the job.'

The 51-year-old Dein, like Sugar, is a self-made man who epitomises the Thatcherite culture. Pushy, but smooth and engaging with it, he initially made his money in partnership with his brother importing exotic fruit and vegetables and selling them from a market stall in west London, eventually moving upmarket as a sugar trader and commodities broker with offices in Pall Mall. Prior to his joining the Arsenal board, he was known to the club as being among the more well-heeled of their loyal supporters, and as a friend and confidant of their leading players. He fitted into that scene perfectly. As one writer observed, Dein, with his youthful, tanned appearance and beautifully cut designer suits, looks more likely to be found at Annabels nightclub than he is in the staid, conservative environment of the Highbury boardroom.

So it is not just being in the company of many of his fellow chairmen that Hill-Wood has experienced something of a culture shock. Working with Dein has been a new experience for him, also.

For example, Dein's friendship with the Arsenal players – maintained when he became a director – was disconcerting to a board who believed in keeping their distance. While Hill-Wood and Dein both deny Terry Neill's suggestion that the latter's relationship with key members of the Arsenal squad undermined Neill's own position – and even led to his dismissal – they were both aware of the pitfalls of such a situation. 'It's a mistake when chairmen and directors get too close to players,' Hill-Wood said. 'David definitely made a mistake on that – he was told that he had made a mistake. Whether he has totally taken that on board or not, I don't know.'

Dein suggests that there is a thin line between being too close to players and too remote from them. 'When we're away abroad, we would often take the players out for a meal or something as a group. We like the dressing-room spirit to be right and that's what it comes down to. In recent years, there have been a number of times that we have not been the best team in a match, technically, but have won because of our spirit and camaraderie. I confess that I might have been too friendly with some of the players – Graham Rix, Tony Woodcock and others – but this was an inherited situation. I got friendly with them before I joined the board, so once I had become a director, what was I going to tell them? "I'm sorry, but I can't be friendly with you? I can't talk to you?" I agree that there has to be a sort of Chinese Wall between players and directors, but I just couldn't cut them off. For me, it was a gradual process of erosion.'

The reverse has been true with his emotional bond with Arsenal. When he became a board member, one observer, referring to his obsession with the Gunners, described Dein's appointment as tantamount to a lunatic taking over the asylum. The more he became involved in the club's affairs, the more his wife, Barbara, was moved to suggest that going into Highbury each day had the same sort of appeal to him as that of a drunk working in a brewery.

Dein had started following Arsenal at six ('The first match I saw was against Burnley when Tommy Lawton scored with a bullet header,' he recalls) and eventually found himself watching not only the Gunners' home first-team games, but also their home reserve matches. In certain ways, the latter gave him as much excitement as the former. 'The thing I remember about the reserve games was that there used to be a little ginger-haired boy who would be responsible for keeping the crowd informed as to how the first team were doing by recording every goal on the scoreboard. If he was running, you knew it was good news, whereas if he was walking, with his head down, you knew it was bad news.'

Bad news for Arsenal has always been bad news for Dein. 'True football fans are brand fanatics,' he argues. 'Whereas people will change the brand of their car, cigarettes, beer – and even change their wife occasionally – they never ever change their allegiance to their football club.'

For Dein, it is an allegiance which is all-consuming – so much so that before our interview, he insisted on my undertaking a guided tour of Highbury and a visit to the club museum.

'With me, the role I have at Arsenal isn't just full-time, it's full-time day and night,' he said later. 'Much to my family's chagrin, I don't switch off even when I am on holiday. I spend so much time on the telephone on club business that I come back with one ear whiter than the other. I mean it.'

Referring to his fantasies of being an Arsenal star himself – during his teenage days he played in a Jewish Sunday league – he says, tongue in cheek: 'I still think I can play. In fact, I have a cartoon at home, a present from Barbara, which depicts me wearing a No. 12 shirt. It's got "The Ultimate Reserve" on it. I am still waiting for that call that never comes. Do you know, I have never ever trained with the Arsenal players or even kicked a ball on the Highbury pitch? Being in the position I am in, I wouldn't do it, but it hurts me. Oh, I'm as frustrated as hell. I am bursting at the seams every match, I am kicking every ball. Whoever sits next to me must end up with bruised shins – I think Barbara could do with shin pads.'

This might partly explain why Dein's office at Highbury is furnished with a weird table whose legs are replicas of those of David Rocastle, the former Arsenal and England midfielder. It was a birthday present from Barbara, and Dein says: 'Although directors shouldn't have personal favourites among their players, it is inevitable that you do. Immediately I saw Rocastle playing for our youth team at 16 I was convinced he was going to be a great player. I couldn't stop talking about him, so Barbara got a friend in the furniture business to make the table for me.'

If Mrs Hill-Wood wanted to give her husband such a gift, she would probably plump for a table with the legs of Tony Adams or one of the Gunners' other solid, dependable, defensive types. 'We've had our flair players, but our success has always been built on our defence,' Hill-Wood said. However, the chances are that Mrs

Hill-Wood would not dream of getting her husband something to remind him of Arsenal. Although he, too, has a love affair with the club, it is rather more laid-back and dispassionate than that of Dein. For example, Hill-Wood does not deem it essential to be at the Gunners' away games. 'I used to go to every match,' he says, 'but that was before I got married and had children. You are not terribly popular at home when you are away watching football every Saturday and playing golf on the Sunday, so something had to give.'

For Dein, nothing can compare with the 'buzz' he gets when Arsenal win. But Hill-Wood said: 'I don't think it is necessarily healthy to be blinkered. Chairmen, directors, do take football more seriously than they did, but this is not always a good thing. Football is actually supposed to be entertainment and fun. I mean, I get very keyed up when watching Arsenal's matches, but I don't go into a dead sulk if we lose because I accept that you are not going to win all the time. I've been saying this to David Dein and other people here – I've told them: "For God's sake, don't get over-excited when we win the Championship a few times because we are also going to go through periods in which we win absolutely nothing."'

This is just one reason why having other sources of income helps. The introduction of Dein's talents came at an important time for Arsenal. It has cost them more than £20 million to turn Highbury into an all-seater stadium, incorporating a new state-of-the-art north stand – a transformation which meant the club's ground capacity being reduced initially from 42,000 to 34,000. He singles out the redevelopment of Highbury as his most stimulating challenge: 'We had an imbalance – we had 28,000 standing positions and about 16,000 seats. Most other clubs had more of a 50:50 ratio.'

He is equally enthusiastic about development of the commercial side of the club. 'When I came here, we had a club shop which my secretary described as a Manchester bus shelter. Today, we've got three big stores, including one megastore at Finsbury Park with 5,000 square feet of selling space. I believe that this part of the business, the whole commercial side actually, will grow indefinitely. There is a limit to how much we and other clubs can take through the turnstiles – all we can do is have a sell-out every game. But the money we can take from TV, from sponsorships, from retail, from mail order, from advertising . . . it's unlimited.'

One suspects that the Dein-led transformation of the club into a dynamic football business (and remember, we are talking about a club which for years deemed it vulgar to have advertising hoardings around the ground and kept faith with a police brass band for its pre-match and half-time entertainment while others were plumping for pop music blaring down the tannoy) has not been an entirely comfortable process for Hill-Wood. He himself dropped a hint in that direction when we met by talking about Arsenal's gratefulness in having someone with Dein's dynamism to 'bully' them.

Dein's philosophy, he said, has stemmed from his experiences of watching sport in the United States. His wife is American (as is Hill-Wood's) and he explained: 'My direction was always geared to what was going on in the States. My wife and I used to go there two or three times a year and we always made a point of going to see the baseball games at the Joe Robbie stadium. It was fascinating to watch the way they marketed the team, the comfort, the way the fans were entertained. I felt that, if English football was going to have a future, it was essential that we started thinking along those lines.'

One of Dein's ideas from the States (with which Hill-Wood admits to being less than enamoured) is the facility which enables Highbury fans to see interviews with the players and play-backs of match incidents on two jumbo-sized video screens. 'We have our own TV studio here,' Dein enthused. 'A fully blown TV studio which pumps the film taken by our own cameras onto the screens.' They cost Arsenal £2.5 million and at the time of their meeting Dein admitted: 'We don't earn money from them, all we do is defray some of the costs by renting them out. It's all about entertaining the fans. Instead of watching Ian Wright score three goals and then go home and see it again on TV, why shouldn't they see it here?'

Hill-Wood, though, remained unconvinced. 'Sometimes, the fan in David takes over to a certain extent,' he said, almost with the air of a father talking about a son who has just gone out and bought an impractical sports car. 'I did not agree with the screens at the start, and frankly I still don't. I know they're an attractive facility to have and it's fun to watch replays of the goals and so on, but I don't see that they make much sense commercially. They cost us £2.5 million, and the running costs are about £250,000 a year. It was thought that we would get advertising revenue from them and hire them out to other clubs, and other sports events like Test matches and horserace meetings. But we haven't got as much back as we anticipated. For example, one of them was hired to Blackburn for one match, but out of the £10,000 fee, it cost us £6,000 to transport it. It's hardly worth it. The good thing is that we are paying for them over five years and I suppose that once they are ours, the pain will be less. But they are never going to be self-financing, which was supposed to be part of the plan.'

By the start of the 1995–96 season, the more positive aspect of the 'Arsenal fan' in Dein rising to the surface could be seen in the players the club had signed, notably Dennis Bergkamp for £7.5 million – £5.5 million above the previous record transfer fee paid for Ian Wright from Crystal Palace just three years earlier – and David Platt for £4.5 million. This outlay was not as lavish as it might have seemed. Arsenal made £6 million by selling Stefan Schwartz and Kevin Campbell and, according to Hill-Wood, had 'roughly the extra £6 million in the bank'. It was the wage-bill for these players which created the most anxiety, not least because it forced the club to raise their salary levels for the other players by more than 30 per cent.

It was suggested in some quarters that Arsenal had to do this, just to bring their players' pay packets up to the same level as those at other clubs. But Dein insisted: 'The image of Arsenal as poor payers was a fallacy. If you take the whole of our squad into account, we have probably been the best payers in the game for some time. Our wage structure is based on three bands relating to the senior professionals, middle professionals and youngsters. We don't believe in paying individuals 200 per cent more than anybody else – we think it is unfair because you need all 11 players to work together and play with a good heart. So when Bergkamp was signed, the band levels had to be raised.'

Arsenal are by no means the only ones who felt obliged to take this route to success. The pressure on the big clubs to extend themselves financially, sparked by the push that Jack Walker's millions gave Blackburn, was best illustrated by Newcastle's £26 million spending spree on new players. Newcastle's accounts up to July 1995 showed an increase in their wage bill from £5.6 million to £8.4 million. That, of course, was before they added such mega-earners as Les Ferdinand, David Ginola, Faustino Asprilla and David Batty to their payroll, not to mention Alan Shearer in the 1996 close season. 'This is where the problems of running a football club come,' Hill-Wood told me. 'We are gambling that we are going to sell out every match, that we're going to have a run in one of the cup competitions and that we are going to get back into Europe. We are gambling on all sorts of things happening – there are times when you have to.'

This was a new direction for Arsenal. In some ways they had been spoilt under Graham, whose early years as manager had coincided with a group of excellent young graduates from the club's youth system all being ready for first-team football at the same time. So, as with Manchester United, whose crop of exciting Old Trafford youngsters helped the club pip Newcastle for the Championship in 1996, Arsenal's need of imported stars had been less pronounced than it was among many of their rivals. This situation, though, changed when the nucleus of Arsenal's Championship-winning team of 1989 began to fade; and one of the criticisms levelled at Graham was that he had become too set in his ways by that time (and perhaps too easily seduced by his ability as a coach to get the maximum out of teams with limited technical skill) to perform the expensive surgery necessary to offset the problem.

It seems strange that Graham's approach to the transfer market was so conservative with a man like Dein in the background. Dein, while insisting that he has never tried to put pressure on managers to buy players, has not been a shrinking violet either. He and Ken

Friar are the members of the board who have the closest links with their managers, with Dein, as one would expect of someone of his youthful energy, taking the more active role in the footballing side of the club. In the aftermath of the Graham affair, that role, particularly with regards to foreign transfer deals, has become more pronounced than ever.

This, though, was an increasingly sensitive point with Graham's successor Bruce Rioch, sensationally sacked by Arsenal little more than 12 months after taking over, and himself replaced by the French coach Arsene Wenger – reportedly a friend of Dein.

For some time, tabloid stories on Arsenal had intimated that the relationship between Dein and Rioch was following the same volatile pattern as the one between Scholar and Burkinshaw at Tottenham. During the season, this was highlighted by Rioch's reaction to a report that Dein, apparently advocating the infusion of younger players in the Arsenal side, had taken it upon himself to go to watch a couple of young Frenchmen. Under the tabloid headline 'Keep Your Nose Out', Rioch was quoted as saying: 'David Dein doesn't speak for me, he will never speak for me. I sign the players and I went to see Sheffield United. I am not interested in [the players Dein went to see].'

The rumours of a growing rift between Rioch and the Arsenal board were given further credence by the remarkably long delay in the manager pledging his future to the club through the signing of his contract. (Ironically, he did not do so until a week before he was sacked, just five days before the start of the season.)

One of Rioch's problems at Highbury concerned his relationship with some of their big-name players, notably striker Ian Wright, the Arsenal fans' idol. On the basis that managers differ in their tactical ideas and ways of motivating teams, it was always going to take time for Rioch to get the same support from Arsenal players that had been given to his predecessor. As far as Wright was concerned, the striker had been used to going forward for balls played into the space behind opposing defenders, thus maximising his scoring potential, whereas Rioch wanted him to put a greater emphasis on coming back and involving himself in the build-up play. It was said that Rioch, the strong-minded and occasionally fiery son of an army sergeant-major, and Wright had some personality clashes, too; indeed, at one point in the season, Wright asked Arsenal for a transfer, a request rejected by the board. Perhaps more revealing was that amid the furore created by Rioch's departure from Highbury, Wright publicly backed the decision – and made a point of telling fans not to blame Dein for the situation.

In view of the 'Arsenal fan' in Dein, he would have been as alarmed as anyone that Wright did not seem particularly happy under Rioch's management. His own relationship with Rioch was not all sweetness and light either. Many felt that Rioch, a member of the Old School of football managers, was hampered by his lack of experience of being in charge at a big club. He was previously manager of Bolton, where he had been able to involve himself fully in transfer market business, and it seems clear that the more he was denied this opportunity at Arsenal, the greater the rift between him and the board became. Hill-Wood was quoted as saying: 'There were a lot of things underneath the surface that we were not happy with. The non-signing of the contract was annoying, but not the main reason. I would say that Bruce's lack of communication with us was the big reason. He hardly talked to us. We did not know what was going on or what his thoughts were, and that is not healthy.'

While all Arsenal's main rivals spent heavily in the transfer market to improve their team during the 1996 close season, Arsenal's only signing had been goalkeeper John Lukic on a free transfer from Leeds United. But Hill-Wood insisted: 'Bruce gave us a list of players [he wanted to sign] and the names were impressive. But you cannot sign world-class players if their clubs will not sell. In a way, it was an impossible task he set us.'

But it was Dein who appeared to take much of the post-Rioch flak. Following the sacking of Rioch, and the news that Wenger had been lined up as his replacement, Steven Howard wrote in *The Sun*: 'Wenger also happens to be a friend of Dein's, which must be a surprise to those who did not realise that the Arsenal vice-chairman had any . . . Now it emerges that Rioch submitted the names of 29 players he was interested in to the board. To get none of them is failure on a grand scale.'

The most intriguing insight into this mess was provided by Mihir Bose in the *Daily Telegraph*. He wrote: 'The language that divided Rioch and the board was the question of transfers. This dated almost from his first day in charge. Rioch had wanted Alan Stubbs and Jason McAteer. He not only valued the players but, like all new managers, felt that these two, his best and most trusted players from his old club, Bolton, would be his voice in the Highbury dressing-room – a bridge to the prima donnas of north London.

'In the traditional English transfer system, Rioch would have spoken to his Bolton successor, and a deal would have been struck. But after the George Graham "bung" scandal, Arsenal set up a new system. Rioch recommended the players, giving his valuation, and the deal was done by David Dein, the vice-chairman, and Ken Friar, the managing director. In general, Friar spoke to English clubs and Dein to foreign clubs. Bolton informed Arsenal that Stubbs and McAteer were not for sale. When they eventually went to Celtic and Liverpool respectively, Rioch was not amused. He was even less amused when he asked for Andrei Kanchelskis and was told by Dein that his friend, Manchester United's Martin Edwards, had made it clear United would not sell him. Soon, Kanchelskis was on his way to Everton, and Rioch began to feel that the new Arsenal transfer system was not working.'

By way of a stinging parting shot, Bose, referring to Arsenal's inability to unveil Wenger as their new manager immediately, on the grounds that the Frenchman was under contract to Grampus Eight and that the Japanese club had insisted on his being held to it while a successor was found, added: 'In a sense, Arsenal have managed the news better than they did in a similar situation ten years ago. Then, during the 1985–86 season, they signed Terry Venables, who was with Barcelona, to replace Don Howe. Nobody told Howe, the news leaked and Howe resigned. Venables did not arrive, and Arsenal eventually signed George Graham, who went on to become their most successful manager.'

Rioch must have known before he took the Arsenal job that he could never hope to win the power that Graham had. Moreover, it is difficult to think of anyone in football who would react to the thrill of a big-player chase with greater gusto and single-mindedness than Dein. One of his fondest memories concerns his trips to Aberdeen with Don Howe, to run the rule over Gordon Strachan, a player both men felt could inject the midfield flair that Arsenal lacked. Even in those days, Dein was not naïve enough to believe that all such moves could be made in secrecy. Nonetheless, it came as something of a disappointment to him when, as he and Howe were boarding a plane to Aberdeen, the stewardess said to them: 'Hi – you two up to see the wee man again?'

The thrill of the chase for Bergkamp was inevitably the most stimulating of all. The big question is: whose idea was it to go after him, Dein's or Rioch's? 'The manager, in our view, must always identify the players he wants to buy, and the directors take over from there,' Dein told me. 'So, if Bruce Rioch comes to us and says: "I really would like to have Dennis Bergkamp and David Platt," right, say no more, we can act. In this case, he gave us a shopping list of eight to ten players and we said: "Leave it to us – we will deliver who we can." He had no involvement whatsoever in the financial negotiations. His only involvement with the players at that stage was to explain to them how he envisaged their fitting into his pattern of play, the roles he had in mind for them.'

The trail leading to Bergkamp began with Dein remarking to Rioch that European clubs had been alerted to the possibility of the brilliant Dutchman being released by Inter Milan. 'Oh, I'd love to get a player like that, or Roberto Baggio or David Platt – someone of real quality,' Rioch had mused. Dein makes the next steps sound equally matter-of-fact: 'Inter had just been taken over, so I sent a fax asking who dealt with transfers there. They came back and gave me the names of two gentlemen. I said: "I want to talk to you about Dennis Bergkamp." They said: "Fine," and it progressed from there.

For the next couple of days, we had chats on the phone, and then they came over, Bergkamp's agent came over and the whole thing was settled quite quickly. There were two meetings going on simultaneously – one to agree the transfer fee and the other, in which Bruce was involved, to thrash out Bergkamp's personal terms. It started at 9 a.m. and we were able to have a press conference announcing the deal at 4.30 p.m.'

But what about reports that Arsenal paid over the odds for Bergkamp? That a few months earlier Newcastle could have had the player for £5.5 million? Even more embarrassing to Arsenal was the comment from Graham that he himself was offered Bergkamp for around £5 million, through an agent, but pulled out of the deal when told the Dutchman's wages.

Dein was unmoved. 'We don't fly by the seat of our pants here,' he insisted. 'It is a very sound operation, and every financial decision is thought through. Had Inter Milan asked for £10 million or £12 million, we would have said no way. We heard about the figure you mentioned [£5 million], but I have to tell you that Bergkamp wasn't going to go there [Newcastle] and I don't believe that he would have been sold at that level in the end. Certainly, Inter Milan's starting point to us was about £8.5 million. You have to remember that the market had moved on [since Inter had initially offered Bergkamp for sale]. Barcelona and a couple of other European clubs had moved in on the act, plus there was the fact that Inter had started negotiating with Manchester United to buy Paul Ince for £7 million, and wanted to make sure that the income from one deal would cover the expenditure for the other.'

As for Bergkamp's £1 million signing-on fee, on top of his £20,000 a week salary, Dein explained: 'Part of the deal was that we were in control of his image rights. He is a big name throughout the world, and we have been able to [benefit from] that. If he wants to do an advert for Ford motor cars, or McDonald's hamburgers, we are in control of that; we control his commercial potential.

'But that's only a small part of the income we hope to get back from him,' Dein added. 'He is on a four-year contract and, obvious-

93

ly, the biggest return on our outlay will come from our performances and achievements on the field.'

Bergkamp's first season in England was encouraging if not startling – Arsenal did not win anything but on the last day of the Premiership campaign, he and Platt scored the goals which enabled the Gunners to beat Bolton 2–1 and qualify for the UEFA Cup.

Peter Hill-Wood was too much of a gentleman to rub salt into anybody's wounds, but it must have amused him no end to note that one of the chairmen who had badly wanted to reach this lucrative money-spinning target, but failed, was Alan Sugar.

Significantly, Sugar was conspicuous by his silence at the start of the following season, when Arsenal – seemingly in greater turmoil than ever as a result of their managerial upheavals and the revelations by Tony Adams about his drink problem – were described as the 'laughing stock' of football.

FOUR

The Thrill of the Chase

One aspect of Graham Sharpe's job as public relations and press officer of bookmakers William Hill is to generate publicity for the company through quoting odds for off-beat bets. Few of the wagers in which he has become involved have been as unusual as the one he almost took on in the late 1980s. The bet concerned a present Football League chairman; and even when he thinks about it now, Sharp, a keen football fan, is inclined to go weak at the knees.

He recalls: 'I was approached by this guy, who was in his early 30s, who said that he had once been a youth-team player at a league club but had been forced to call it a day at that stage in his career because of injury. He said his wife was writing a book about will-power and dieting, and as a stunt to publicise the methods she had recommended, he wanted to back himself to play league football. I was amazed: although he claimed that he had not played seriously for more than ten years, at amateur level, the only bet he said he was interested in was that he would play in a First Division match, and that if he did so, he would win £500,000. We checked him out as thoroughly as we could, and as far as we were concerned, it was a safe bet for us. The only problem was that to make it worth while from our point of view, we had to get some publicity out of it; and because the prospect of what this guy thought he could do was so remote, I felt that the media would just look upon him as a crank and ignore it. So I proposed that, while we would accept the wager, we would grade it by also offering odds against his appearing in matches at lower levels.'

Sharp was about to put the details in writing to his client when, while reading the newspapers one day, he saw the man's photograph alongside a story about a businessman who had made a bid to take control of Manchester United. 'I thought: "My God, I recognise you",' Sharp recalls. The man was Michael Knighton.

Knighton, of course, was unsuccessful in his attempt to become the new United boss. But Knighton, who has since taken over at Carlisle, certainly showed that he lacked nothing in confidence – and football skill. To this day, Sharp, like millions of others, still remembers those famous television shots of Knighton giving the Old Trafford crowd a pre-match treat by juggling the ball on the pitch with the dexterity of George Best. Sharp also remembers the feeling of horror – and relief – that engulfed him when, shortly after the news of Knighton's involvement in United became public, he received a telephone call from him. 'Well, the cat's out the bag now,' Knighton said. 'I suppose it's too late for that bet?'

'Yes,' Sharp replied.

'You've had a lucky escape,' Knighton reminded him. 'I can tell you that, if you'd taken the bet, I would have got Alex Ferguson to play me as a substitute in an end-of-season game.'

Knighton is not the only chairman who provides a particularly vivid picture of the club figurehead as egotist and frustrated player. When it comes to fantasies, they are no different to any balding suburban middle-aged man who, having watched a James Bond movie, might drive his family saloon out of the local cinema carpark as if it were a Ferrari. Professional football, though, is a particularly powerful creator of dreams. Watching players being hugged by grateful team-mates after scoring an important goal, and receiving gladiatorial acclaim by a packed crowd, can do strange things to onlookers – especially to those who have never been good enough

Look what money can buy: Jack Walker, whose millions transformed Blackburn Rovers, celebrates their 1994–95 Championship success (Empics)

The Old Trafford dynasty: Martin Edwards (right) took over the chairmanship of Manchester United from his father Louis (left) (*The Guardian*)

Edwards and Michael Knighton, the man to whom he nearly sold his shares for £10 million. No doubt Knighton's broad smile reflected his anticipation of what those shares would be worth today (*The Guardian*)

Arsenal's Peter Hill-Wood, one of the game's 'gentlemen' chairmen
(Bob Thomas Sports Photography)

David Dein, Arsenal's new-style entrepreneurial vice-chairman (*The Guardian*)

LEFT: On the way out: Norwich City's Robert Chase after another broadside from the Carrow Road supporters (Rob Howarth)

RIGHT: Peter Johnson, one of the 'migratory' chairmen. He switched his allegiance from Liverpool to Tranmere and then to Everton (Empics)

BELOW: Crystal Palace's Ron Noades, a qualified coach and referee – and far more than merely a club figurehead (*The Guardian*)

ABOVE: Sir John Hall and his Newcastle kingdom (North News and Pictures)

LEFT: One of the big guns north of the border: Rangers chairman David Murray (left) with manager Walter Smith (Empics)

RIGHT: Irving Scholar, one of the trailblazers for the new breed of football chairmen (Empics)

Chelsea's Ken Bates (right) and his fellow director Matthew Harding during a ceasefire in their tense relationship (*The Guardian*)

to be professional footballers themselves, and for whom no amount of success in business could bring anything like that recognition.

No doubt, psychologists would have a field day with men like Knighton, and Gillingham's bespectacled 40-year-old chairman Pat Scally, who registered himself as a player with the club towards the end of the 1995–96 season in the hope of getting into the action for their last Third Division match at home to Scarborough. It had been ten years since Scally had last played the game seriously, as a member of Heston United, a Sunday league team from south-east London. His motivation for wanting to do so with Gillingham was a £20,000 bet that he would appear in an Endsleigh League match for at least ten minutes, and the cost of sending the Gillingham players – who had clinched promotion to the Second Division – on a summer holiday to Barbados. But Scally, like Knighton, was thwarted. Gillingham's manager, Tony Pullis, refused to play ball with him. 'No chance, not in a million years,' he said, referring to the fact that Gillingham, while having been pipped for the Championship by Preston, were in a position to establish a new lower-division record for the fewest number of goals conceded in a season (which they did).

Scally and Knighton would undoubtedly have attracted much jealousy from some of their fellow chairmen had they achieved their targets. Among those one might place on that list are Doug Ellis, who claims to have played a few matches at inside-forward for Southport – mainly in the reserves – during the war, and Ken Bates, who overcame the disability of a club foot to play for Arsenal juniors but was forced to quit the game as a result of a motorcycle accident.

Ellis does not deny that he is a frustrated player. 'I just love football – I'm devoted to it,' he says. 'I did try to be a professional footballer. I come from the Wirral, and in the late 1930s I trained at Tranmere Rovers two nights a week. I used to have to travel nine miles there on my bike, but I never made the grade really. I was a box-to-box runner; I was fitter than anybody else and worked harder than anybody else, and yet I just didn't have the necessary pace and natural technical ability.' Still, the one consolation for him now is that, in terms of skill, he can at least show other chairmen and club officials a thing or two.

When we met, the latest addition to the memorabilia and mementoes that adorn his plush office at Villa Park was a plaque that had been awarded to him at the annual FA Council Congress the previous summer – his reward for beating some 40 other council members in a penalty competition. 'Graham Kelly [the FA's chief executive and a former goalkeeper] loves to get into his tracksuit and jump about,' Ellis says, hardly needing to add that he himself, though in his 70s, found it equally enjoyable trying to get the ball past him. What made his spot-kick triumph so uplifting is that he was the oldest competitor. 'All the others in that competition were younger than me – there wasn't anybody within 15 years of me,' he recalls proudly. 'But I don't miss penalties.' He thinks about it and beams: 'I could still do it, and honestly, there was nobody within 15 years of me . . .'

But if there is one chairman in the Premiership and Football League with good cause to fancy himself as a potential matchwinner, it is Manchester City's Francis Lee, the 52-year-old former City, Derby and England striker who led the consortium to take over at City from Peter Swales in January 1994.

In a career spanning 16 years, Lee, strong and quick and bursting with self-confidence, made more than 500 league appearances and scored 228 goals. With the likes of Colin Bell and Mike Summerbee, he was one of the attacking stars of the swashbuckling Manchester City team which won the Championship, FA Cup, League Cup and European Cup-Winners' Cup under the management of Joe Mercer and Malcolm Allison between 1965 and 1971. Few players of his generation could match his charismatic appeal. Noted for his quick-wittedness and his one-liners, Lee was very much an entertainer.

Right from the very start of his career, Lee left colleagues in no doubt that conventional barriers meant little to him. Gordon Taylor, who has known Lee since he was 16, the age at which he and Lee began their careers together at Bolton, recalls: 'He was always confident. I had lunch with him on my first day on trial with the club and he asked me if I was going to sign for them. Remember, Bolton were a prominent club then – they had just won the FA Cup in 1958 – and I just said that I hoped to do so. But he said: "Well, I am. I have seen the first team, and they are rubbish – I will be playing for them this season." He did – he made his début for them at 16.'

Bolton's manager then, Bill Ridding, would have found Lee's personality even more disconcerting. Taylor goes on: 'We went down to play the double-winning Tottenham side, and on the train journey, Bill, who'd had a finger shot off in the war, put both hands up to show that we would be getting a £10 bonus if we managed to win both points. Franny shouted: "Come on, boss, let's get it right – what are we on, £10 or £9 and a half?"'

Taylor laughs, just as Lee did when, on asking Ridding for a pay rise once, he was told: 'You should take whatever you can get, otherwise you could easily end up digging ditches for a living.' In addition to the success he achieved at Manchester City, Lee made doubly sure this was never going to happen to him by showing the same positive attitude that hallmarked his playing career as a businessman.

He had started the ball rolling even at Bolton. 'I used to go to the local technical college in the afternoons,' recalls Taylor. 'One day Franny says to me: "Why are you bothering with all that schooling?" I explained that I had promised my mum and dad that I would not forget about my education once I became a professional player, and Franny said: "Look, forget that – come in with me. I'm going to get waste paper, have it reprocessed and resell it. We can be partners." I said: "That's not for me. In any case, I have enough trouble getting on with you on the pitch." Imagine what I felt like a few years ago when I read that Franny had sold his business for millions,' winces Taylor.

By the time Lee retired as a player at the age of 32, the soft tissue manufacturing business he had started was turning over some £8 million a year. By then also embarking on a successful career as a racehorse trainer and owner, Lee eventually sold the company for more than £8 million, with the new owners, Hazelwood Foods, installing him as chairman of this newly acquired subsidiary and also giving him a seat on their main board.

It is possible, if not probable, that some Manchester City players and the manager at the time, Brian Horton, must have viewed Lee's takeover of the club with trepidation. 'It must be very comforting for the players to know that you have seen everything,' he said ominously. 'It must be disconcerting to some. They can't kid me. If a guy isn't giving 100 per cent for the team, I can spot it in five minutes.'

The strange thing about all this is that, for all Lee's football knowledge and experience which he passed on to his players through the advice and encouragement he gave them during his pre-match dressing-room visits, City ended the 1995–96 season as one of the Premiership's relegated teams, along with QPR and Bolton. To the public, the fact that Lee had inherited a number of problems from the previous boardroom régime (such as having too many players whom the club could not get rid of because of the lucrative contracts they were on) counted for less than some of his perceived mistakes. Among these was the sacking of Horton and the appointment of Alan Ball as his successor. Many felt that Lee was too easily influenced by his memories of what the game was like when he and Ball were at their peak; by the pair's mutual respect as England team-mates at a time when the technical standards and application of such stars was as high as they have ever been in the post-war years. But the game had changed a lot since then, as Ball often acknowledged with his critical comments on the subject; and, more pertinently, Ball's managerial track record before he moved to Maine Road was far from impressive.

As if City losing their Premiership place was not hard enough to take for their fans, in a season in which Manchester United achieved the Championship-FA Cup double, Lee and City continued to attract ridicule at the start of the following season when the club parted company with Ball, and clearly struggled to find anyone with better managerial credentials willing to take his place. The first man they approached was George Graham, but Graham, though anxious to return to the game since the end of his 12-month FA ban in May, turned them down because he was unhappy with the salary offered and the lack of funds available for new players. At this point, even the most partisan Maine Road follower might have been moved to accept that City's image as a club with more potential than most had become a myth and, indeed, that City were in no less of a mess under Lee than they had ever been under his predecessor.

In some ways, however, a lot of chairmen would have gained considerable satisfaction from Lee's struggle, not because they didn't like him – how could anyone not like 'Franny Lee'? – but because it proved to them that their involvement in the game, their so-called 'meddling' in matters said by the professionals to be beyond their comprehension, was justified.

One area in which they have assumed a particularly dominant role is that of transfer deals. This in itself has been difficult for some managers to accept. After all, if you want to buy something special in Harrod's, going into the store and doing so yourself is much more fun than letting someone else do it on your behalf. Some managers also have mixed feelings about whether their chairmen are in the best position to get the best deals.

In that respect, it would appear a lack of inside football knowledge – a naïvety about the culture of top-class professional footballers and the eye-for-the-main-chance element in their make-up – certainly caused Alan Sugar to be caught out in the case of Jürgen Klinsmann. Sugar's expertise as a businessman counted for little in the hard-nosed and cynical football-business world inhabited by stars such as the German international. Sugar had been hailed as a hero – and rightly so – when, aboard his luxury yacht in the South of France, he signed the outstanding World Cup striker for Spurs for £2 million in the summer of 1994. It seemed the perfect antidote to the depression that had descended upon Spurs following the FA's decision to deduct 12 points from their 1994–95 league total and ban them from the FA Cup. Despite being a regular member of the German team, the highly accomplished Klinsmann, then just turned

30, had hit a flat spot in his career at club level, and a move from Monaco to a top club in England, where the game was much more competitive, was viewed as the ideal challenge for him. Sugar, who signed Klinsmann on a two-year agreement, clearly felt confident that he had the player where he wanted him. 'Jürgen's not greedy like some,' he pronounced. 'He is the most honest player I've met.' But after his superb first season at White Hart Lane, when he was voted Footballer of the Year, Klinsmann exercised a controversial opt-out clause in his contract to sign for Bayern Munich. Although the German club bought Klinsmann for the same figure Spurs had paid for him, Sugar tried unsuccessfully to get UEFA to force Bayern to pay more, and was left moaning that Tottenham had been used merely as a stepping-stone for the player to end his career on the highest possible note financially.

There was some sympathy for Sugar in the English game. One chairman says: 'The galling thing for Alan is that Klinsmann would probably have done even better in his second year at Tottenham. In hindsight, what Alan should have done once he'd won his battle with the FA over the punishments they'd meted out to Spurs, is to have sat down and negotiated a new deal with Klinsmann. But he didn't and, as it turned out, he fell for the five-card trick. I can tell you — foreign players are the cleverest of the lot. They and their advisers come up with all sorts of different things in contract negotiations, all sorts of clauses to their benefit, and you've got to be wise to this.' Scholar's failure to do so on that occasion hardly did much for the credibility of chairmen as astute professional football people.

The view that chairmen were taking on more than they could handle was further reflected by Sugar's remarkable outburst against Klinsmann during an interview on BBC TV's *Match of the Day* programme. 'Here's the last shirt [Klinsmann] wore for Spurs, against Leeds,' Sugar said. 'He's written on it: "To Alan, with a very special thank you." I'm bloody sure it's a very special thank you, I'm the blooming mug that relaunched his career.' Sugar then tossed the shirt aside, and added: 'I wouldn't even wash my car with it.'

Despite what happened at Spurs, none of the league's longest-serving chairmen would have been put off by Sugar's experience. Among those who took delight in being in the thick of the transfer-market action was Norwich's Robert Chase, a man who had no doubts that he could do better on this side of the game – at least in financial terms – than any manager. There was some justification for that confidence. To Chase, the basic principles of buying and selling players were little different to those of buying and selling houses or cars, much to the chagrin of Norwich fans and managers. Before his much-maligned reign at Carrow Road was ended by popular demand at the end of the 1995–96 season, Chase, who used a red file box as a briefcase – does that not tell you something about his business-like approach? – was certainly no slouch when it came to selling his stock at good prices.

He denies reports that, during the early part of his Norwich chairmanship, he hired a sports marketing and publicity company to enhance some of his players' images and thus their transfer-market appeal. 'Not true, but nearly right,' he says, explaining that he merely used a sports agency to produce stories about players suggesting that the club 'might' be prepared to let them go.

The sale which he was really able to get his entrepreneurial teeth into was the British record £5 million transfer of striker Chris Sutton to Blackburn in July 1994. With the touch of high-finance profes-sionalism and élan that the deal merited, Chase undertook a whistle-stop tour of prospective buyers by private plane. He recalls: 'It was just a little two-seater out of Norwich Airport, and we had hire cars standing by at all our landing points. The overall cost was something like £1,400 or £1,500 but I think I saw everybody who had inquired about Chris [Manchester United, Liverpool, Blackburn, Arsenal and Tottenham] in one weekend.'

In addition to that £5 million transfer fee, which the club wanted paid in one go, Chase was also insisting on two sell-on clauses in the deal – that Norwich be given a 25 per cent cut on the next transfer fee to be paid for Sutton, and 50 per cent of the one after that. 'So that there would be no misunderstandings, I wrote everything down regarding what we were looking for and more or less read from a script,' he told me. 'I just said: "This is what we are prepared to do, this is how we want to do it and these are the terms I am prepared to accept."

'At Manchester United, I spent more time waiting for Martin Edwards to get up to his office in the lift than I did actually talking to him. I told him what we wanted, he said it was too much money, and I said: "Right, thank you Martin, goodbye." Simple as that. I then saw Peter Robinson [Liverpool's chief executive] and he was much more interested. But he wanted to talk to his colleagues before giving me a definite yes or no, so it was straight on to Blackburn. It did not take them long to agree to what I wanted – I remember we went to a restaurant, and by the time I was halfway through the melon I'd ordered, they'd said yes.' That was Arsenal's response, too. 'Once we had two clubs in that category, I knew we were away,' Chase said. 'Once I got two people to agree to meet our asking price, I could have raised it a bit. But I didn't. I played it dead straight. Five million is what we asked for and five million was what we got.' Sutton eventually chose Blackburn.

By the time the curtain came down on Chase's controversial ten-year spell at Carrow Road, Norwich's total player sales had edged towards the £30 million mark. As one of our interviews for this book coincided with the allegations concerning managers lining their own pockets from their clubs' transfer deals, it seemed reasonable to ask Chase whether chairmen, having started to play a more active role in this aspect of the game, might also be vulnerable to temptation. 'The only thing I have ever been given – the only gift I have ever been offered – from the transfer deals I have handled was from Walter Smith [Rangers' manager] when I sold Dale Gordon to him [in 1992]. We'd been negotiating the deal, in a hotel at Heathrow Airport for about three hours, and eventually I signed the contract, he signed the contract, and he gave me his pen. "There you are, keep it for good luck," he said. The pen couldn't have been worth more than three or four quid – it was a posh biro – and it was as if he was saying to me: "You drive such a hard bargain that you might as well take my bloody pen as well." I've still got it.'

Mark Bowen, the former Norwich full-back, says Chase was a master at getting the better of players in contract negotiations. 'I always felt that, before I came to see him, he'd probably spent hours thinking about what I was going to say, and how to respond to it. He had an answer for everything or, if he didn't, he'd move the goal-posts and tie you in knots that way.'

Chase himself alludes to this when recalling the signing of Efan Ekoku from Bournemouth. 'He brought his agent, Mel Stein, up here, and I met them at seven at night, before a reserve-team match at Carrow Road. I thought we were going to do the deal before that game, but no, it went on until 11 at night, and then we had to adjourn. I said: "Okay, we'll continue tomorrow – let's start at 6.30 in the morning.' Ekoku's jaw dropped a bit, but I knew when they came back that they wanted to do a deal. Half the art to this is guessing what the other side are going to do. As a matter of fact, when we started again the following day, we didn't pick up from where we'd left off the previous night – we started from scratch again. I just kept walking them around and around the table – it was quite exhausting but it worked in our favour because I've never known anyone to get as confused over what he wanted as Ekoku was. We eventually got the whole thing settled at 5 p.m., and he actually accepted less than I had offered the night before.'

The signing which stands out the most in Chase's memory was that of Robert Fleck from Rangers in 1988. 'David Stringer [Norwich's manager] had tried several times to contact Graeme Souness [then Rangers' player-manager] to buy Fleck. Suddenly, early one afternoon, David rang me to say that Souness could see us and could we get to Glasgow that evening? I got us booked on a mail plane; David and I sat in a cargo plane. Rangers had a match that night, so we watched the game and when Souness came out of the shower I was introduced to him in the dressing-room corridor. The conversation could only have lasted 35 seconds, and was conducted on the move, as we were walking through the corridor. I said we were interested in buying Fleck; he said he wanted a million; I said I was prepared to go to £400,000; he said we should split the difference; I said: "No – £500,000 is my very last offer." He turned around and said: "Done." He did not stop walking; he didn't even shake my hand. He said: "Take him away," and when I raised the subject of necessary paperwork, he replied: "We'll do it tomorrow." That was it.'

Could Stringer not have approached Souness instead, manager to manager? 'David Stringer couldn't have done it,' Chase argues. 'When Souness asked for a million, David would not have been quick enough to say £400,000. I'd never met Souness before and I am sure he thought I was going to crumble. I mean, he was one of the big stars of the football world and I was a twopenny-halfpenny boy from Norfolk. But I stood up to him. When I say that David couldn't have done it, I mean that he is not as mentally quick as me in certain ways. He is twice as quick as me in the football sense – ten times quicker than you and me in thinking about football – but when it comes to money . . .'

This is a song that most chairmen sing nowadays. Doug Ellis sums it up by recalling his dealings with Jim Gregory (then QPR's chairman) over the transfer of Villa striker Mike Ferguson following a match between the two clubs at Villa Park. 'Mike had been told not to leave the club after the game, but when we sent for him he was nowhere to be found. We spent all night trying to track him down – it was about two in the morning by the time we were able to make contact with him – and all this time, Jim Gregory and I were in the boardroom. I'll never forget it. I said: "Jim, you've got your chauffeured car outside – why don't you go back to London and leave it to Les Allen [QPR's manager] to tie up the deal?" He looked horrified. "Because it's my effing gelt," he said.'

'In the old days, there was not a great deal for club chairmen to do,' says Ken Bates. 'Everything could revolve around the team manager and the club secretary. Just take the stadiums – you did not have the Football Licensing authority, the Safety of Sports Ground Act and things like that. Did you know that every club director is legally responsible for the safety at his ground? That in itself concentrates the bloody mind a bit, let alone all the other responsibilities involved in running a top football club these days.'

Bates recalls an incident at another club where one of his fellow chairmen, a man not noted for holding back when it came to anybody spending his money, was told by his team manager: 'It's my job to run this football club, and it is your job to find the money.' The chairman retorted: 'It is my job to sack you – you're out.'

Bates chortles, and adds: 'What we do at Chelsea – and I am sure it is done at a lot of other clubs – is that we all sit down at the end of the season, we look at the likely profit that we feel we are going to make and at what our financial commitments are, and we then say to the manager: "You've got X amount, plus whatever you bring in from outgoing transfers." Any club which is properly run will do this, rather than allow the manager to walk in and say: "I want to buy Charlie Bloggs for £8.5 million, can you raise the money?"'

For years, Bates argues, chairmen and directors wilted under this pressure and relied heavily on the goodwill of the banks for their survival. 'I remember getting into an argument about this with the late Dr Richard Grossmark [Gillingham's chairman and a member of the Football League management committee] as many as 20 years ago. I said: "The sooner clubs start living in the real world, the better. You think that the rules that apply to other businesses don't apply to football clubs – rubbish. One day, the banks will bounce club cheques. They will become tired of being emotionally blackmailed by clubs, the apparent threat of losing 50,000 accounts if they put a club under. They will wake up to the fact that the 50,000 accounts from the club's supporters are mainly ones that they could do without anyway."'

His friend, Ron Noades, continues the theme: 'Kids who are good at football don't work at school, right? What makes me laugh about our game is that very few of our players go on and get degrees or anything like that. Probably 98 per cent of the players became professional footballers without having had a particularly good education, without even having passed their 11-plus. Suddenly, from that exclusive group, we select our managers and then we expect them to deal with contracts and transfers.'

Such arguments are sound enough in principle. But at what point should the pride that chairmen have in themselves as businessmen encroach into areas such as evaluating football talent, team selection and tactics? It brings us back to the question of that football ego-factor – the feeling that if a number of chairmen can't keep in touch with their fantasies of being on the field with their teams, the next best ego trip is to involve themselves in the worlds of their managers and coaches.

Bates, with Hill-Wood the joint second-longest-serving Premiership chairman behind Ellis, echoes the views of most of his colleagues when he insists that there would be little point in his pressurising a manager to put his own ideas on players and the game into action even if he wanted to do so. 'If you want to buy a player and the manager doesn't want him, you are wasting your time,' Bates says. 'The manager either won't pick him, or he'll hold him back by not playing him in his best position or something like that. So I don't interfere, but I can think of a number of players whom I have wanted to buy – against the judgement of the Chelsea manager of the day – who have gone on to make big impacts at other clubs. For example, Gary McAllister and Dean Holdsworth when they were with Leicester and Brentford.'

Noades nods in agreement. 'Not one single manager can say that I have interfered with his team selection,' he insists. 'I don't usually ask what the team is because I don't want to give a bad reaction. No way do I want the manager to feel that he has to pick a certain player just to please me. I want the manager to pick the team he wants to pick.' But Noades, who was previously in charge at Wimbledon (before they joined the league) also agrees with Bates that the football knowledge of a chairman, and what he can contribute to the playing side, is often underestimated. Indeed, the Crystal Palace supremo, who has an FA coaching badge and refereeing qualifications, is acknowledged as the most football-orientated of all England's club leaders. Much of his time is spent evaluating potential stars of the future. He is out watching matches most nights; if there is a game going on anywhere in the south of England, you can bet that no matter how minor it might be, and whatever the weather, Noades will be there.

He suggests that all the matches he sees, combined with his coaching background, make him no less of an expert on the game than some of those who have earned their full-time living from it. One man who will readily concur with this view is a 69-year-old Scottish gentleman by the name of Jack Steedman, one of the five members of his family on the seven-man board of Clydebank FC. He has possibly been even more involved in the day-to-day running of his club than Noades has been. The former president of the Scottish League and chairman of the SFA's International Committee, Steedman and his older brother Charles formed Clydebank 30 years ago, after eight years as owners of East Stirling. Though he was never a league player himself, the ubiquitous Steedman is renowned for the number of football responsibilities he has taken on. Like Noades, he has an insatiable appetite for scouting in the most unlikely environments, and for the buying and selling of players. Despite employing a first-team coach, he has even selected the team and given players tactical instructions.

When I met him once he told me: 'The reason I pick the team is that it would be an intolerable position if I knew a club were interested in buying one of our players, and the manager left him out or substituted him.' Was he any good at it? 'Well, I should be – I've had more than 30 years' practice. I have probably selected more teams than anyone else in Britain.'

Noades has not gone as far as Steedman but says: 'I think that what Len Shackleton said in his book about directors knowing nothing about football was probably true then but it is not true now. Most of the chairmen I meet today know quite a lot about football and the supporters know a lot as well. I mean if you want to scout for a player, you go out and ask a club's fans: "Who is your best player?" and they will tell you. I think I have a reasonable ability to judge players, particularly young players. You meet a lot of people in football who are good judges of players but find it difficult to assess how a kid might develop. You know, it's a question of anticipating how they are going to develop physically as well as technically. I enjoy that side of it.'

To his credit, Noades's record in that department is impressive. Crystal Palace is where Stan Collymore started his league career. True, Palace, who signed him from Stafford Rangers, offloaded him to Southend; but, as far as Noades's judgement is concerned, it is significant that the contract contained a sell-on clause that brought Palace a slice of the player's £2 million transfer fee when he moved to Nottingham Forest. Among the players to have established themselves as top-liners at Palace from the lower ranks, and thus been sold by the club for considerably more than they cost, are Geoff Thomas, Ian Wright, Mark Bright, Chris Armstrong, Chris Coleman, Gareth Southgate, Richard Shaw and John Salako.

Notwithstanding the question of where Palace would be now if they had curtailed their selling – which Noades deems essential to balance the books and ensure the club have a sound financial base from which to keep growing – his track record in the wholesale-retail transfer business is certainly impressive. He is at pains to point out that he and the Palace manager, coach and chief scout work as a team and that, though he will often push the manager in the direction of a player he likes, the final decision is the manager's. However, once Noades is certain of a player's capabilities, he is a difficult man to argue against.

One illustration of this concerns Geoff Thomas, the tenacious midfielder who was bought from Crewe for just £250,000. Noades recalls: 'I must have taken Steve Coppell [then Palace's manager] to see Thomas five or six times before he finally agreed to buy him.' Noades had originally been alerted to the player's potential when he saw his performance as a substitute for Crewe at Aldershot. 'I phoned Dario Gradi [Crewe's manager] about him right away,' he recalls. That was something of a mistake because, according to Noades, he did not know then that Thomas was only on loan to Crewe from Rochdale – and Gradi did not tell him. 'He went and signed him instead,' Noades says. Still, he continued to keep tabs on the player. 'Palace had a match at West Bromwich Albion on New Year's Day, and Steve and I drove up to Lancashire afterwards to watch Stockport against Crewe that evening. Thomas did not win one bloody tackle or header, and I did not need to ask Steve whether he thought he was worth buying.' However, Coppell did eventually see the light and Thomas became one of Palace's most influential players.

As if to underline that he does not exert his authority as much as some might think, Noades says that it was mainly due to Coppell's influence that Thomas was eventually sold to Wolves for some £2 million less than what Palace might have got for him from Blackburn. 'We should have sold Geoff Thomas for £2.8 million but didn't because Steve didn't want to sell him and I backed him up. My weakness, really, is giving managers too much leeway in buying and selling. Crewe had to be given a cut of any sell-on fee for Thomas and I said to Steve: "Look, there must be a price that you would accept for him." He said: "I'll accept £2.5 million clear after Crewe have been paid." I would have needed to get £2.9 million out of Blackburn for that. At the time, we were poised to buy two Wimbledon players, Robbie Earle and Terry Phelan, for £3.8 million, so I went to Sam [Hammam, Noades's successor as Wimbledon owner] and asked if he'd come down to £3.7 million. He said no. Blackburn were not prepared to increase their fee for Thomas from £2.8 million to £2.9 million and Crewe refused to take £300,000 instead of £400,000, so the deal fell down.

'In the end, of course, we ended up with £1.1 million. You could turn around and say that I should have overruled Steve and you're quite right. That has been par for the course for me, really.'

Only once, Noades claims, have Palace bought a player without the manager seeing him. That was striker Chris Armstrong, who Noades signed from Millwall for an initial fee of £1.1 million in 1992.

'I only saw him once before deciding we should make a bid for him. Really, you should watch a player half a dozen times. Usually, a scout recommends him, then he is watched by the chief scout and the manager. If the manager likes him, he discusses it with the board. We're fortunate here – we don't have to go through that process. If I am out with the manager or chief scout we can decide there and then if we can do it. Steve never saw Armstrong. At the time, we needed a full-back as well as a striker, so Steve went to Notts County and Alan Smith [then his assistant] and I went to see Millwall against Orient in the Cup. I knew he was the one we should buy after just ten minutes, and I spent the next 80 minutes thinking about what sort of deal we could do with Millwall. The following morning, Thursday, I got Alan to see Steve at our Mitcham training ground to persuade him that we should buy Armstrong – which he did – and I made contact with Reg Burr [Millwall's chairman], who was in Florence.'

Noades had some stiff competition, ironically from Wimbledon's Hammam. In view of Wimbledon's position of having to move from their old ramshackle Plough Lane ground and use Palace's Selhurst Park stadium for their home matches, the manner in which Noades pipped Hammam in the Armstrong race must have been little short of demoralising for his Lebanese pal. Hammam had already made a bid for Armstrong but, as he also wanted to buy Chris Coleman from Palace, he suggested to Noades that he would not go 'too strong' for the former if he could get the latter. 'I did not want to sell Coleman then,' Noades recalls, 'but while Sam and I were talking to each other on the phone at lunchtime on the Friday, the fax from Burr confirming Millwall's agreement to sell him to us was coming through.'

At this point, even Armstrong did not know that the two clubs had agreed terms, let alone Hammam. 'He played for Millwall on the Saturday, and he was told after the game that he had an appointment to see me on the Sunday. I told his agent what we were going to offer, got the contract typed up, and he signed it on the Sunday.'

But what about Hammam's agreement concerning Coleman? 'He did not have an agreement,' Noades says. 'He was just suggesting it.' He shrugs and adds: 'I think he would have gone to £750,000 for Armstrong. We went to £1.1 million, so we knocked him out on the price, really. I did not want any long-winded negotiations involving the two of us which would just have pushed the price up.

I just went straight to a figure that I knew Reg Burr would accept. With add-ons, it came out at £1.3 million, and then they got another £600,000 [as a result of Armstrong making 30 first-team appearances for Palace], so they ended up with £2 million for him.'

But when Palace sold Armstrong to Tottenham in 1995, they received £4.5 million — the sort of deal that inevitably causes Noades to scoff at the view that men like him lack 'professional' football expertise. 'All the word "professional" means in football is that you earn a wage at it — it's not like being a chartered surveyor, is it? A lot of players who go on TV to analyse a match don't know what they are talking about. You could get people at boardroom level to go on and they would be able to discuss a game just as well. They don't have the credibility — they are always being told they know nothing about the game — but I know lots of directors far more knowledgeable about football than some of their players.'

More knowledgeable than some of the managers, too? 'Well, I wouldn't say they know more than the manager. If that were the case, they would have known eff-all to have appointed him in the first place.'

All of which brings us to the records of men like Noades when it comes to their managerial changes — which, to the game's professionals, is the most common guide to the level of egotism (and football knowledge) among the men who run England's clubs. Dave Bassett's appointment as Palace manager towards the end of the 1995–96 season brought the number of managerial changes under Noades at Palace to eight in 15 years — or ten if one takes into account that when Steve Coppell returned to the club in June 1995 it was in the all-embracing position of 'technical director', and that the first team was mainly the responsibility of coaches Ray Lewington and Peter Nicholas. Most of these men were sacked by Noades. Ken Bates, who took over at Chelsea a year later than Noades assumed control at Palace — in April 1982 — has a similarly impressive managerial sacking record. Prior to Ruud Gullit, his managers were John Neal, who retired through ill health; John Hollins, Bobby Campbell and Ian Porterfield, who were dismissed; David Webb, who did not have his contract renewed; and Glenn Hoddle, who left to become England coach.

Bates is sensitive about the view that he has been far too ruthless. When you ask him what his biggest mistakes have been, he replies: 'Funnily enough, not being ruthless enough.' By way of example, he draws your attention to Hollins, who was Chelsea's manager when they were relegated to the Second Division in 1988. One bone of contention between the two men concerned Ernie Whalley, who was Chelsea's coach and who, according to Bates, antagonised players through adhering to methods that were too abrasive and too heavily weighted in favour of the physical side of the game. As it turned out, Bates, weary of Hollins's refusal to sack Whalley, did the deed himself and brought in Bobby Campbell as coach, apparently without even seeking the manager's agreement. Hollins had been one of the most popular players in Chelsea's history and was a figure who commanded enormous respect in the game. Not surprisingly, Bates's attitude towards him brought the Chelsea chairman a storm of abuse in the media. Even in one reference book about managers, containing the backgrounds and records of all the men to have filled this position in the League since the war, the authors felt it necessary to comment on how Hollins's authority was undermined. Hollins, they wrote, 'was perhaps treated rather badly by Ken Bates'. Officially, Hollins 'resigned', but if ever there was a case of a manager being pushed into it, it was this one.

But Bates still refuses to accept that he was wrong. He was once quoted as saying, 'Hollins has a strong wife – maybe I should have appointed her as manager.' During our interview, he told me: 'I should have sacked Johnny Hollins long before I did – I left it too late. Had I done so, we would not have got relegated.

'The view that I interfere on the playing side is a great myth,' he continued. 'To people who claim this, I say: "Well, give me an example." They say: "Oh, you sacked Ian Porterfield." Not before time [Bates has been quoted as saying that, in his opinion, Porterfield was more of a No. 2 than a No. 1]. "You sacked David Webb." Well, I did not sack him; he served a 90-day contract and we did not renew it. We wanted someone different – better.' He reminded me that Webb had sold Graeme Le Saux to Blackburn for £575,000, adding that Le Saux had gone on to become a key England player. He has been equally blunt about Campbell, the other manager he axed: 'A strong man, right for the time, but he probably went past his prime with us,' he has been quoted as saying.

True to his confrontational nature, Bates also bristles when you suggest – gingerly – that men like him are on an ego trip. Nonetheless, he clearly enjoys the rapport that he has established with the fans, and his fame. No chairman has had as many newspaper articles written about him as he has. The walls of his office at Stamford Bridge are covered with photographs of him, and many caricatures and cartoons relating to the controversies in which he has figured. 'How many other chairmen are signing autographs for other clubs' supporters?' he says. 'I've had more photographs of me with a Liverpool scarf draped around my neck than Kenny Dalglish. For one match at Everton [the game to mark the centenary of the Football League] I actually had a group of Everton fans dragging me into their section so that I could watch the match with them. They were going to get me drunk, fix me up with a bird – it was a gas.'

Noades insists that he would hate this. 'I get pissed off sometimes when I think of how much money I could have made had I not been running Palace all these years. People just think that it's an ego trip for me. But the truth is that I am quite shy, really. I don't like meeting people – I probably get accused of being rude for that reason – so being the centre of attraction is not for me. I am only interested in football.'

Still, whatever the truth behind this, Noades and Bates are no different to others when it comes to occasionally giving off negative signals. One needs only to refer to him by his nickname – 'Deadly Doug' – for most football followers to immediately know who one of the others is.

FIVE

Deadly Doug and Blaster Bates

When you meet Doug Ellis, the first thing that strikes you about him is his charming, urbane manner.

'I like him,' says one experienced football journalist in Birmingham. 'I once ran a local boys league and Doug gave up virtually an entire evening to make the end-of-season presentations. He was tremendous with the lads – I remember that one was quite cheeky to him, but Doug, far from taking umbrage, actually invited him to come to Villa Park for a trial.'

With me, too, Ellis oozes bonhomie, laced even with flattery: 'I see, Jason, that you know your football.' Give him a compliment back, praise for some of the up-and-coming youngsters in his reserve and youth teams, and he seems almost humble. 'Oh, I am charmed, I am charmed. Thank you.'

So how does one reconcile this picture with the fact that Ellis, in addition to that famous nickname of his, has also been referred to in the media as 'The Chairman from Hell'?

The silver-haired, distinguished-looking Ellis, who became Villa's chairman long before any of his counterparts today took up this position with their present clubs, has a reputation for being the most egotistical of the lot – and also the most trigger-happy in that gory business of firing managers. For those searching for clues to these characteristics, the personal number plates on Ellis's Rolls-Royce read 'AV1', and the plaque on the desk of his sprawling Villa Park office bears the message 'Beware – my mood is subject to change without notice'.

Though it would be unfair on him to suggest that he had anything to do with choosing the recording of the Nat King Cole song 'Unforgettable' for the Villa Park telephone switchboard system, his image as a man who enjoys fame and recognition is endorsed to some extent by his fellow chairmen. Some take delight in openly teasing him about it, none more so than Peter Johnson and Ken Bates.

Johnson and Ellis, both Wirral men, are keen sailors, and Johnson – every bit as competitive as Ellis and with an acute sense of how to find the latter's Achilles' heel – seems fond of winding him up with such comments as: 'I captain my boat; he has a crew. His boat was bigger than mine at one time but now I've got a new 92-footer – and his, well, it's off the shelf and I can put it on my trailer.'

Johnson claims that he once had to 'rescue' him. 'We were heading for Sardinia, for the 1990 World Cup, and I decided to slip my lines about midnight with the intention of getting into Sardinia at ten or 11 the next day. It was then that I picked up a distress signal from Doug on the radio. A nail on his boat had sprung, water had seeped in, and of course as soon as they'd put on power, all the water went down to the stern, where his cabin was. I could see him about three miles off the port side, and we came up alongside, picked him up – we left his captain and my crewman aboard – and he sailed with me.

'He was in his mid-60s, not young enough to be diving into the cold Mediterranean at midnight,' Johnson continued, no doubt getting pleasure from the prospect of my recounting this story to Ellis. 'Half of Birmingham hated me – the Aston Villa supporters, of course.'

Talk to Bates about Ellis's remarkable transformation of Villa Park into one of the best stadiums in Europe, and he will remind you that one of the stands bears his name. Ellis's supporters maintain that he deserved that honour. They claim that the stand was built for £1.8 million less than major construction companies had quoted through Villa taking charge of the operation themselves under Ellis's guidance. But Bates, one of the few whose experience as a chairman dates back even further than that of Ellis (he was originally in the position at Oldham, between 1965 and 1969) goes through with his digs at Ellis just the same: 'You know they're building a new stand at Villa Park now?' Bates says, pausing to give his punch-line maximum effect. 'They're going to call it "The Other Doug Ellis Stand". When I rib him about the one there already, he says: "Nothing to do with me." Nothing to do with him? He forgets to mention that his son is on the Villa board, as are his doctor and his solicitor.' Bates warms to the theme: 'He is always talking about himself, how he has built up his business,' he continues with an unmistakable hint of affection. 'I say to him: "Doug, you must be tired – let me tell the story. I know it better than you do by now."' Bates shakes his head and grins. 'The thing about it is that he doesn't realise you are taking the piss. You just can't get under his skin.'

The more time you spend with Doug Ellis, the more you notice that he does talk about himself a lot; and, perhaps equally significantly, he drops into the conversation the names of all manner of distinguished people with whom he has been associated. In Britain, they don't come much bigger than John Major, whom Ellis describes as a 'friend'. He shows you a letter from him ('I got it only last week') and adds that the pair have much in common.

'I'll tell you a story about him which you ought to get published,' Ellis says. 'I said to him one day, a long time ago when he was Chancellor of the Exchequer: "Have you moved into No. 11 yet?" He said: "I have, but Norma [Mrs Major] hasn't – she's back in Cambridge." I said: "But you didn't go to Cambridge, John," and he said: "Of course not, I left school at 15."' Ellis then recounts a lengthy discussion with Major on how the latter built himself up from humble beginnings, and especially how he studied for his degree in economics through correspondence courses while working for two years as a motorway construction labourer. 'You see, I'm likening him to me now,' Ellis says. 'John Major rose from the position of parliamentary backbencher to Chancellor in ten years. Not a bad record, is it? The point I am trying to make is that the man is streetwise. People don't realise it – I mean, if you have worked as a labourer, living in Portakabins all over the country, you do get to know something about life, don't you? I would love to be his PR officer. I can relate to John Major, you see. I know what it is like to rough it.'

Like Major, Ellis is very much a self-made man. He comes from a farming family. 'But we had no money,' he says. 'My father died when I was three and my sister was eight weeks old, and my mother never remarried. My mother did all kinds of things to get us through school. She had Parkinson's disease for the last seven years of her life – she died at the age of 85 about ten years ago – but at least I had been able to give her something back and make things as comfortable as possible for her. My background made me determined to work for myself, to get into a position where my family need never be vulnerable or short of a bob or two.'

It was during his own National Service, in the navy, that Ellis first hit upon the idea of how this might be achieved. 'I think that one of the reasons I did well was that I was a good listener,' he says. 'In those days, when we were stationed in the Far East, I would listen to the conversations of the chaps on the lower deck. In addition to the usual two things, beer and sex, they would talk a lot about the places we were in and how one day they would like to bring their girlfriends or wives back. I thought: "There's business here."' So Ellis elected to go into the travel business, a step which led to a massive travel conglomerate – the third biggest in Britain – comprising 12 retail agencies and seven tour-operating companies at the airports of Gatwick, Luton, Birmingham, Manchester, Glasgow, Belfast and Dublin. He was described as 'a prototype Freddie Laker', an assessment he readily endorses. The 'personal information' about him, supplied by Villa, states that he is 'recognised as the pioneer of the package-holiday industry in the provinces in the early 1950s, when he was chairman and owner of such well-known travel companies as Mato, Global, Sunflight, Jetway, Ellis Travel, with a total staff of 300 and offices in Canada and Spain.'

Ellis, who sold all his travel companies in 1976, recalls: 'Compared with others at the forefront in this field, I was the little boy in the provinces and they were the big boys. But I made more money than them. After four years of war service, I had come out of the navy with a £300 gratuity. That's all I had. I started from nothing, and I have got to be proud of that, haven't I?'

He also made a lot of money from a wide variety of other businesses, including building and construction, a brewery, a string of butcher shops, shoe shops, cafés and insurance broking agencies. Nowadays, he is the chairman of the Ellis Group of Companies, Ellmanton Construction Company, Aston Manor Brewery Company, and he holds the position of Lloyds Underwriter. The long list of his charitable activities includes his chairmanship of the Good Hope Hospital NHS Trust. In football, too, he appears to have a finger in every pie. He is an FA Council member as well as a member of the FA International Committee, the International Football League Board, the FA Finance Committee, the FA Charity Shield Distribution Committee; the Centres of Excellence Central Liaison Committee and the FA Technical Control Board.

All this has unquestionably stood Villa in good stead, although Ellis is understandably sensitive about the view that he himself might have benefited from his involvement in the club. Despite the inevitable criticism over the fact that his construction company's workforce has been used to put some of the club's ground development plans into operation, Ellis maintains that it has meant losing money rather than making it. In addition to the comparatively low cost of building the Doug Ellis Stand, he draws your attention to the first 18 of the club's 95 lucrative executive boxes; the first stage of his masterplan to increase the club's income. These were built in 1969, and Ellis recalls: 'It took me three board meetings to convince my colleagues that they would be advisable, even though we would have to lose 9,000 standing positions to accommodate them. I said: "They won't cost the club anything – I'll get them built by my own company and you can pay for them after three years from all the rent you will get for them." Some people actually complained – they said I had made money out of the club. In fact, for one reason or another, the boxes eventually cost me considerably more than I took for them.

'When I got involved with Villa, I walked away from making many more millions in my own business. I devoted my time to Villa completely; for many years, I did everything for nothing.'

To put it another way, even a businessman as formidable as Ellis can give the impression of having a soft spot when it comes to football – the one area of his life in which his public standing can be easily measured. Does the type of criticism he might get from the Villa faithful hurt him? 'Yes.' Truthfully? 'Yes, it does, no doubt about it.' Because you want to be loved? 'Yes – who doesn't?'

On that basis, he admits that he can still get quite emotional over the memories of the surprise 70th birthday lunch that friends organised for him in 1993, a bash which attracted almost 500 guests and some of the biggest names in football. John Major – who else? – wrote the introductory message in the brochure to mark the occasion and Ellis even had Tommy Docherty and Jimmy Greaves, two of his most outspoken professional critics, there to pay homage to him. He was even seen to shed a tear when Tom Finney, his boyhood idol who became a neighbour and close friend during a period when Ellis lived in Preston, made his entrance. He would have been in an emotional state again in 1996, when the bitterness that Villa's fans directed at him the previous season – as a result of their team coming close to being relegated and Ellis sacking Ron Atkinson, one of the most charismatic of his ten managers – was suddenly turned into a tidal wave of adulation as Villa finished fourth in the Premiership and won the Coca-Cola Cup.

Unfortunately for Ellis, such high points have not been common during his involvement with Villa, as chairman of the club, since 1968. As might be indicated by the fact that he has had three different spells in that position, and was involved initially in a considerable measure of boardroom blood-letting, examples of what his critics describe as his streaks of 'ruthlessness' have not been hard to find.

Before his arrival at Villa Park, he served a three-year 'apprenticeship' as a Birmingham City director. 'It gave me the finest lessons I could have had on how not to run a football club,' he recalls. 'I have said that many times. The big problem at Birmingham was that the board was made up of three different families – they'd been associated with the club for donkey's years – so there were three different factions. There was no unity amongst them.' But it wasn't long after Ellis's arrival at Villa Park that the same could be said about the boardroom there.

When Ellis took over in December 1968, Villa, who had been relegated to the old Second Division the season before and who were struggling to hold their own even at that level, were not in the best position financially. 'The club were bankrupt – we shouldn't have been operating as directors, really,' Ellis says. He tackled that problem by lending Villa £100,000 (with the option of converting the money into shares) and initiating a new issue the following year. 'I asked 8,336 shareholders to buy one share each at £5. I said: "The board would not have more than 35 per cent, so with your 65 per cent, you can come to our annual general meetings and tell us how to run the club." All wonderful socialist principles – although as time went by, I found out that it just doesn't work that way.'

By August 1972, Villa, having slipped into the Third Division, had regained their place in the Second. But Ellis, despite having been generally perceived by the fans to have done a good job, was deposed as chairman following a no-confidence vote in him by his boardroom colleagues – and was even asked to relinquish his directorship. At the root of this sensational turn of events was a personality clash between Ellis and Harry Parkes, a former Villa player who had been on the board for some 30 years. It was suggested that Parkes, and other directors, felt Ellis had been taking too much of the credit for the improvement in Villa's fortunes. This, however, did not cut much ice with many Villa shareholders, especially those with memories of the rousing public speeches Ellis had delivered when asking for their moral and financial help four years earlier.

Thus, at an EGM, Ellis was voted back into the chair and Parkes lost his place on the board. For those absorbed in political battles, there were more riveting episodes to come.

In September 1975 Ellis resigned as chairman and was succeeded by Harry Kartz. There was nothing political about the move on this occasion, he says – he merely needed to devote more time to his businesses. But at the end of 1979 Ellis became embroiled in another scrap, this time over a dispute with Villa's major boardroom share-holders – Ron Bendall and his son Donald – concerning their accumulation of more shares than he deemed healthy for the club. Reports indicated that the Bendalls had acquired 21 per cent of the shares and, according to Ellis, this contravened the principle behind the pledge he had made to prospective Villa shareholders in 1969. When his battle with Bendall reached fever pitch, he was quoted as saying: 'With over 8,000 shareholders, more people have a say in the running of this club than in any other sporting organisation in the world. But the only way the Bendalls' investment can be safe is to buy more shares so they can control the club. Once the Bendalls have an absolute majority, Villa's democracy is dead.'

Looking back on it now, Ellis reflects: 'When I gave the club the £100,000 loan, I said I would only take it back when they had returned to the First Division and had half a million in the bank. But I still had the option to convert the money into shares – so, although I was no longer chairman, I was still in control.

'As far as Ron [Bendall] was concerned, well, I'd made a promise to the shareholders. I said, "Ron, what are you going to do about it?" He said: "Nothing." So I called an EGM and we agreed that if I won I would buy his shares, and if he won he would buy mine.'

Ellis lost ('I got 42 per cent of the votes, he got 44 per cent'); and, apart from a short spell on the board at financially crippled Wolves, where he helped mount a rescue operation that helped save the club from extinction, he spent the next three years in football exile.

By the end of 1982, Bendall, who had become Villa's chairman, was in poor health and living as a tax exile on the Isle of Man. Villa, despite having won the Championship in 1981 and the European Cup in 1982, were showing signs of sliding again. More disturbing was the fact that they were under investigation by the Fraud Squad. Ellis was prompted to give Bendall a call when he was told that he had sold out to a consortium led by Harry Parkes. The information proved false. 'Ron confirmed that he had received an offer from Parkes, but had not yet accepted it. "Does that mean that you can sell them to me?" I said. "Yes," he replied, "as long as you are prepared to pay the price."

'He told me a lie, of course,' Ellis adds, with the air of someone who has long become acclimatised to such tactics in business. 'Harry subsequently told me that he hadn't offered as much as Ron had claimed. The difference was £80,000.'

Still, Ellis had 42 per cent of the shares and was now truly in charge of Villa. And he was in a position to settle some old scores. Among these was the one concerning Harry Kartz, who had been a Villa director for 16 years but who, despite once being in partner-ship with Ellis as a racehorse owner, had stood firmly on the side of the Bendalls when Ellis was jousting with them.

When I spoke to Kartz in November 1994, he recalled that Ellis, upon assuming control, immediately asked him to resign – a request which he refused. When Kartz did reach the end of his road as a director 12 months later, Ellis told him that even if he wanted to continue watching Villa, he would not be getting any complimentary tickets. 'If you had resigned when I asked you, you could have had two directors' box seats and two carpark tickets for life,' Kartz claims he was told.

Strange as it might seem, though, Kartz talked about Ellis with some affection and respect, particularly with regards to the chair-man's assertiveness. He recalled the trainer of a horse they owned complaining that Ellis had woken him with a telephone call in the early hours to discuss why the animal had not won the previous day. Kartz was equally impressed by Ellis's assertiveness when the pair, *en route* to a race meeting in France, were on a plane which had broken down on the runway, and Ellis strode into the cockpit to demand – successfully – that they be transferred immediately to an aircraft in the take-off queue in another part of the airport.

The two had a number of boardroom disagreements. 'But Doug is very clever,' Kartz said. 'He was always in control. While I would lose my temper, he would just sit there quietly and smile.' He insisted that any hard feelings towards Ellis had long since disappeared: 'I don't hold anything against him. Doug is a very interesting man. I admire him. What he has done at Villa, especially with regard to the development of the stadium, has been tremendous. But he is very ruthless . . .'

Some of the directors who have fallen by the wayside during Ellis's reign once had a claret-and-blue tie with the letters KOBE (Kicked Out By Ellis) on it. Though there is unquestionably a much less intimidating side to him, the message is unlikely to be lost on anyone who might be approached for the Villa manager's job.

Brian Little became his tenth manager in November 1994. The others have been Tommy Docherty (1968–70), Vic Crowe (1970–74), Ron Saunders (1974–82), Tony Barton (1982–84), Graham Turner (1984–86), Billy McNeill (1986–87), Graham Taylor (1987–90), Dr Jozef Venglos (1990–91) and Ron Atkinson (1991–94).

To understand why none has lasted long, it might help to know that the only silverware Ellis has picked up during all his years as chairman is the Coca-Cola Cup, won in 1994 and 1996. It must have been particularly galling for him that arguably the greatest two years in Villa's history – the winning of the Championship under Saunders in 1981 and the European Cup under Barton in 1982 – were two of the three years when he was not even on the board.

He is philosophical about this. Perhaps typically, he indicates that even in his absence, he could take some credit for those successes. 'No doubt about it. Seven players in our squad, the total squad, came from our youth scheme. I planned that. In the early days [of his chairmanship], I remember going on TV and saying that our aim would be to breed players rather than buy them. I said: "You people out there — you be the scouts. Tell us about any promising kids in your area and we will at least get someone to take a look at them, and if they are showing anything whatsoever, we'll give them a trial."' So keen was Ellis to ensure that Villa would not lose out in the race for potential stars of the future that when the chief scout went to the homes of youngsters to try and persuade their offspring to sign for Villa, Ellis went with him. 'I did it dozens of times,' he says.

One family graced with the presence of the chairman was Little's. Born in Durham, he signed for Villa as a schoolboy in the late 1960s. Ellis recalls: 'His mum says to me: "Our Brian is very shy, he'll not go away from home I'm afraid, Mr Ellis. Now, if it was our Alan [Little's brother] it would be different — Alan will go anywhere." I said: "Can he play? Is he a good player, too? Would the two come together?" She said yes, so I signed both of them.' Brian went on to become one of Villa's most popular attacking players and gained an England cap, which more than compensated for the fact that Alan never made the grade at Villa Park and was sold to Southend for £8,000.

Gordon Cowans, the influential midfielder in Villa's European Cup-winning side, also came from Durham, from a mining family. 'His mother told me: "Every scout in the country has been here," and I think I said: "Any chairmen then?" When I went to see them, I persuaded them to come down to have a look around the club — I paid for them to come down by taxi.' Mr and Mrs Cowans also moved to the Midlands and they were appointed the stewards of the hostel for the club's young players. 'You have to be careful on that one,' Ellis says, referring to his position in the FA hierarchy and the sensitivity concerning the regulations relating to club inducements to schoolboy players.

Ellis did nothing wrong. But the need for men like him to be seen to be setting a whiter-than-white example has become more pronounced partly as a result of their higher public profile. Football is a competitive business and, even to chairmen, the temptation to bend rules and regulations, or at least to sail dangerously close to breaking them, in order to gain an edge over rivals, can be overwhelming. The late Robert Maxwell was as ingenious as anyone in that department. The regulation that no person could have an interest – shares-wise – in more than one club appeared to be contravened in the early 1980s when he bought a large chunk of Oxford, followed by Reading and then Derby. He was able to do this through spreading control of these clubs between his companies and his family – and, after an unsuccessful bid for Manchester United, he was keen to add Watford to his list. It was at that point that the implications in all this for English football began to rise to the surface, creating one of the biggest furores in the game at that time. The League president, Philip Carter, and David Dein, both leading lights on the League Management Committee, agreed a deal with Maxwell whereby he would be allowed to buy Watford in return for relinquishing his interest in the other clubs as soon as he could. It was a considerable negotiating triumph by Carter and Dein, in view of Maxwell's insatiable appetite for power and his possession of all the legal aces. But other members of the Management Committee overruled them, insisting that it should be the other way round. Maxwell could still have gone ahead with his Watford plans but, to his credit, he had vowed to drop them if he didn't get the Management Committee support, and he was true to his word.

Ellis, too, experienced a spot of bother from the rulebook watchdogs in 1993 when he was summonsed by the Football Association to answer reports that Villa had broken FIFA regulations on the direct involvement of agents in transfer deals when they signed the Australian goalkeeper Mark Bosnich. It led to Villa being fined £25,000. Later, the embarrassment for Ellis was rendered even worse by the increasingly tacky stories about the behind-the-scenes wheeling and dealing between the club figureheads and agents at other clubs. The man involved in the Bosnich deal was Graham Smith, the same man whose company was involved in Teddy Sheringham's move from Nottingham Forest to Tottenham. That transfer, of course, became one of the most controversial in British football history following the revelation that Smith's company had been paid £50,000 by Spurs – on an invoice carefully constructed to circumvent the regulation that agents could not be paid commission on transfer fees – and the court allegation (during the battle between Terry Venables and Alan Sugar for control of Spurs) that some of the money had been earmarked as a 'bung' for Forest manager Brian Clough.

When Ellis appeared before the FA, he might well have argued that Villa's entry into the complicated minefield of agent-influenced transfers was no more questionable than that of many other clubs.

More fascinating to the public, though, is Ellis's defence of his managerial sackings. In that respect, he points out that his 'Deadly Doug' nickname was given to him by Jimmy Greaves, and referred not to his managerial casualty list but to his expertise as a deep-sea angler. He and Greaves, he explains, once took part in a television programme on the sport, and Greaves, impressed by the dexterity Ellis showed in putting his catch out of its misery, exclaimed: 'You're deadly.' Ellis shrugs over the effect that comment has had. 'I've had small boys coming up to me in the street, and shouting: "Oi, Deadly!" But I don't mind – I take it all in good fun.

'If you look at the number of managers I have sacked, I think the average amount of time they were here works out at about three and a half years. I don't think that's too bad. Players do get fed up with the same manager, the same voice, the same routine after three or four years. How many managers at other clubs last longer than that? But irrespective of this, I hate sacking a manager, I hate sacking anyone. I have sleepless nights beforehand. I remember Graham Turner. He didn't really make it here, and the day after we were beaten 6–1 by Nottingham Forest I asked him to come to the house. I knew that we had to part company with him, but it was so difficult. I walked all the way around the garden with him for an hour, tears in my eyes.'

Some managers – if not all – would no doubt find it hard to keep a straight face on hearing this. Take Tommy Docherty and that famous comment about feeling he needed to watch his back when he worked with Ellis. 'The chairman says to me: "Don't worry about our poor results, Tommy – I am right behind you." I says: "Thanks very much, Mr Chairman, but I would much rather have you in front of me where I can see you."'

'I couldn't help but like Tommy Docherty,' Ellis says. 'You should have heard what he said about me at my 70th birthday party.'

He admits, though, that his memory can sometimes let him down. During our interview, he even suggested that I send notes of his comments to him to enable him to check them for accuracy. One subject on which he appeared to be less than sure of his facts concerned the exact number of managers he has sacked.

'You've sacked about seven managers,' I ventured.

'No, six,' he replied. The debate then becomes confusing, and Ellis reaches for the phone to bring Villa's secretary, Steve Stride, into it. 'Steve – how many managers have I sacked? You've heard me call six – do you know how many it is? You tell me the managers I have sacked.' Stride refreshes his memory. 'Docherty I sacked . . . Crowe I sacked . . . Barton was sacked, yes . . . Turner, fine . . . McNeill I sacked . . . Venglos I sacked . . . Atkinson . . .' He puts down the phone and shakes his head. 'That's seven. Would you believe it? I have been saying six and nobody has disputed it.' He pauses, and then gives out another correction. 'I could argue about Venglos, couldn't I? I didn't actually sack him, did I? He came in to see me and offered his resignation.' Ellis does not wait for the obvious reaction about this being a moot point. 'Okay, let's split the difference – let's call it six and a half.'

The two managerial departures which could definitely not be attributed to Ellis were those of Saunders (who was appointed by Ellis but who resigned as a result of a contractual dispute under the chairmanship of Ron Bendall) and Graham Taylor (who left to become England manager).

The dour Saunders, one of the strongest-minded managers, takes a more liberal view of Ellis than others might do. 'Doug and I complemented each other, inasmuch as he seemed to thrive on being in the spotlight, whereas I looked upon it as a pain in the backside. I wanted to run my part of things, whereas Doug seemed to want to run everything. But there was only one real hiccup in our relationship – when he was late for our team coach for my first away match, and I gave the instruction for it to leave without him. He was not a very happy man when he had to get the secretary to give him a lift in his car – he was fuming by the time they caught up with the coach halfway up the motorway. But I think he respected me for it.'

Ellis talks fondly of Saunders; he says he learned a lot from him. 'I have probably learned something from most of my managers,' he says. He likes to think he has had a 'good relationship' with all – 'with the possible exception of Ron Atkinson'.

This, indeed, was probably the most controversial of all Ellis's managerial sackings, given that although Villa were struggling in the league, Atkinson had steered the team to the Coca-Cola Cup – Ellis's first trophy – only the previous season. On the premise that even Villa Park is not big enough to accommodate two figures with such large egos, cynics might well say they saw it coming. Ellis is unwilling to go into details about the reasons behind his decision, but says: 'Ron is a local lad, and I knew him when he was a player – when he was at Kettering, he used to ring up for air tickets. He's not a chap I would necessarily want to go out and have dinner with, but I felt that someone with his flamboyant personality and glamorous image would be good for Villa. But you can't have two chairmen of a football club – and the chairman and the manager must be like blood brothers. That is how I have always operated, but it wasn't the case with Ron, so it was only a matter of time before we parted company. It was not a snap decision by any means. All I can say is that Ron had a good job here, which I am sure he regrets having lost. He was foolish.'

But how many times has that been said about Ellis? Come to that, how many times has it been said to his face? Ellis seems surprised by the question, especially the inference that he rules by fear. 'Let's just say that there is not a single manager who has not been invited by me to tell me straight if he thinks I have said something out of place. I invite them to do it, and they have done.'

Leaving aside the question of what might have happened to some of these gentlemen as a result, it is clear that certain chairmen are more difficult to stand up to than others – some chairmen for whom the description 'street-fighter' might well have been invented.

One obvious contender for a place in that category is Alan Sugar, as Terry Venables has found. You would need a couple of stiff brandies before crossing swords with the notoriously grumpy, aggressive Tottenham chairman; even then, you would still be liable to end up in a lot of pain. The same can be said of the similarly intimidating Ken Bates, a man who seems at his most comfortable when he has something to fight against and can fire on all cylinders. 'I'm a Saggitarian,' Bates once said. 'You know, tilting at windmills, deep sense of injustice, all that sort of stuff. I'm difficult to deal with because I'm not logical.'

A more potent characteristic of his is that the truly fanatical football supporters – and especially those from working-class backgrounds – probably find it easier to identify with Bates than they do with any other chairman. He suggests that this might have something to do with the fact that, apart from recognising that he has the best interests of Chelsea at heart, he is very honest and willing to stand up and be counted on the side of the underdog. As he told me: 'If people ask me a question, I give them an answer. They might not like the answer, but what they see is what they get. I am not like some other chairmen – they are like politicians in their dealings with the public because they don't say anything, they don't take a definite stand or position on anything.'

There are some subjects on which Bates is a closed book. He is defensive – and clearly irritated – when you question him on the personal financial aspects of his involvement with Chelsea ('Let's get one thing straight, I am not prepared to discuss my personal finances with you') and his links with the so-called 'mystery men' who own shares in Chelsea through a remote network of offshore companies. But he makes so much noise in other areas that your interest can be easily deflected from such touchy topics.

At 63, Bates is almost ten years younger than Ellis, but there are similarities between the pair in their childhood experiences and the single-mindedness with which they have made their personal fortunes. Bates himself, born and raised in Ealing, west London, has tended to be uncomfortable when talking publicly about his family background. For all his uninhibited media interviews on football, you have to look long and hard through the massive files of newspaper cuttings to find any references at all to his personal life, his upbringing in particular.

What *is* known is that Bates's mother died when he was in infancy; that he and his father then lived apart; that he was brought up by his grandparents; and that he did not learn he had a sister until he was 16. In one magazine interview in 1990, he said that he did not want to discuss the reasons for this, except to say that his father had a number of wives and live-in lovers. Unconventional it might have been, but the relationship between Bates and his father was seemingly quite strong. 'The old man painted buses for London Transport,' he was quoted as saying. 'He worked bloody hard and he saved up to have my club foot operated on, which in 1938 cost a lot of money. One leg is still thinner than the other, and I have to have shoes specially made.'

In another Bates interview, with Rob Hughes in *The Times* in April 1994, Bates intimated that he had inherited some of his father's traits when revealing that the pair briefly went into a haulage business together but that their competitiveness worked against the partnership. He told Hughes that 'the old man was still competing to the end, that before he died at 86 two years ago, he was still chatting up nurses and dialling 999 to call the police, insisting that the nursing home was holding him against his will'.

The obvious conclusion to be drawn from his formative life experiences is that Bates is a man with an outsize chip on his shoulder. Chris Lightbown of the *Sunday Times*, a journalist who has got closer to him than most, wrote particularly profoundly on the subject of Bates's complicated temperament and personality when he observed: 'He is an outsider who needs to be a winner. But the winner needs to be an outsider.'

There is a clue to this in Bates's opposition to the suggestion that the top clubs in England play too many matches and that there are too many competitions. One would think that Chelsea would feel a greater affinity with the likes of Manchester United and Arsenal on this, but Bates's attitude is more in keeping with the smaller Premiership clubs such as Coventry and Southampton. At the time he won his struggle to increase the old First Division from 20 clubs back up to 22, Bates argued: 'If you listen to Arsenal and Manchester United, all they are saying is that it's a disadvantage for them competing in Europe. What is really being said is that we should reduce the number of games so that the less successful clubs have fewer matches, which will give them even less revenue, which will condemn them perpetually to being poor, while the Big Five perpetuate their stranglehold on soccer . . . I am always told the argument in favour of it [a smaller First Division] is that there would be less football played, which would improve the quality of the game. Well, my answer to that is "bullshit" – the most ardent advocates of smaller divisions can't wait to get on an aeroplane and get jetlagged on the other side of the world, either because the directors want an all-expenses-paid booze-up, or they want to get the money on offer.'

This strong rebellious trait has served Bates exceptionally well in both his business life and Chelsea FC. His business background has been varied and, as with his involvement in Chelsea, punctuated by controversy. He initially made his money quarrying gravel in Lanca-shire, a period during which he had four years at the helm of Oldham. Even in those days, having paid £12,000 for 24,000 Old-ham shares (a huge amount of money then, when the average wage was around £20 a week), he left nobody in any doubt that he was in command. The first of his many brushes with authority came in 1967 when he organised Oldham's summer tour of Rhodesia (now Zimbabwe) at a time when Britain had declared the country's government illegal. 'Mr Bates believes in being part of a committee of two, with one member absent,' one director moaned. Bates then moved to Dublin, where a bank he founded went into voluntary liquidation and he ran into a spot of legal bother. The Bates business venture odyssey moved on to the West Indies (land reclamation), to Australia (sugar planting) and to Monte Carlo (property development) before he returned to England and settled down in rural Buckinghamshire, in a dairy-farming empire in Beaconsfield.

At that point, Bates returned to football. Responding to a request by an old friend, Wigan chairman Freddie Pye, to help him out, he had a short spell as their vice-chairman. But Bates was looking for a club in the south to get his teeth into; and no club in that part of the country was more in need of someone like him than Chelsea, who had been allowed to drift towards insolvency through the self-indulgence of the Mears family – owners who, according to Bates, treated the club more as a hobby than as a business. Though Chelsea's main stand had been rebuilt, in a style which reflected the massive cost of the operation, the rest of the ground was little short of dilapidated. To Bates, the other major problem for the club was that the men running it had created an environment for what he called 'poseurs, hangers-on and fair-weather friends', as opposed to anyone with a genuine love of the club and, more importantly, the expertise and motivation to push Chelsea upwards and onwards. 'The number of people who claim that they love a club, and at the same time screw it . . .' he muses.

Chelsea, whose total debts amounted to around £1 million, were in administration when Bates came along to buy the club in 1982 for just £1 (plus his agreement to guarantee their huge running costs). Within 18 months, though, Chelsea, who had been losing £12,000 a week at the time Bates took over, were starting to make a profit. But that challenge was as nothing compared to what he faced over securing the club's future at Stamford Bridge.

Bates bought Chelsea from the then chairman, David Mears, but not the freehold of the ground – that was owned by the Mears-controlled SB Property Company. Bates could have tried to buy the stadium when he took over the club – it is estimated that he could have had it for £1 million at the time. Instead, he came to an agreement with Mears to lease the ground for seven years, with the option to buy it when the term had been completed, at whatever its market value at the time. Mears, though, sold the stadium to another property company, Marler Estates, who applied for – and were granted – planning permission to build residential homes and offices on the 12-acre site. Not surprisingly, this raised the cost of the land to £20 million. Chelsea's future at Stamford Bridge looked even more problematic in 1989 when, their lease having run out, Marler were taken over by Cabra Estates.

All this was a horrific scenario to Bates, whose vision of Chelsea's future had long revolved around developing the site himself to give the club a big income outside football. It was not until 1992 that his battle to own Stamford Bridge – which he estimates cost him more than £500,000 a year in legal and professional fees – was finally won. Cabra, financially crippled by the property slump, sold Stamford Bridge to the Royal Bank of Scotland, who in turn handed Bates a buy-now-pay-later agreement by which he can take Stamford Bridge off them by the year 2012 for the £16.5 million they forked out for it.

While Bates still talks about Mears's decision as 'treachery', others feel that Bates invited what happened through his public condemnations of the Mears family. Moreover, Irving Scholar, who referred to Bates as the 'Bearded Buccaneer', provided more intriguing food for thought on the matter in his book when he claimed that he had tipped off Bates about Mears's attempts to sell Stamford Bridge to another property company in September 1982. Scholar, who was in the business himself, had not yet become involved with Tottenham at that stage. 'Ken's big mistake was not to buy Stamford Bridge from SB Property Company then,' Scholar claimed. 'I think that the Mears family, though wanting £1 million for it, might have sold it to him for £800,000. Dear old Ken, in his inimitable fashion, offered them £600,000 and they subse-quently sold it to Marler Estates for around £1.2 million.' Though Bates denies this ('I had an agreement with Mears and he reneged on it, it's as simple as that'), Gordon Taylor says of him: 'He's like a lot of powerful businessmen in that if ever you are doing a deal with him, he has to feel he has got the better of it.'

His confrontational manner apart, Bates is looked upon as the chairman with the strongest sense of humour. In part, this helps explain why he is more popular than Sugar. He smiles and laughs more. Outwardly he is everybody's friend. His wisecracks, delivered at the expense of himself as well as his colleagues, have brightened many a meeting of club chairmen and chief executives. At an FA Council meeting, for example, where it was customary to have two minutes' silence for any club representative who had died, Bates is said to have asked an elderly gentleman who had just come out of hospital: 'Do you want your two minutes now?' At a Premiership club meeting, when a debate on the AIDS problem in relation to professional football raised the question of how serious it was outside the game, Bates proclaimed: 'I don't know the answer to that, but what I do know is that I would hate to get this disease again.'

Gordon Taylor sums up this side of Bates when he recalls spotting the chairman in conversation with a group of fans before a match at Wembley. 'He just pointed at me and bellowed: "Hey, lads, don't blame people like me for the rise in football admission prices; it's that bugger over there, and the members of his union, that you should be having a go at."'

Indeed, when Bates is in full flow, he could easily be mistaken for any boisterous, high-spirited fan larking around in the local pub. While showing me the finishing touches being made to the new north stand at Stamford Bridge, for example, he caught sight of a group of workmen inspecting a sheet of metal, and shouted: 'Now I have seen everything – six guys to bang in one nail.' Laughter all round. He approached one member of the group with white hair, and put his hand on top of the man's head: 'I see we have a Spurs supporter among us.'

Later, there was a glimpse of the other side of Bates – the side that has produced 1,001 provocative verbal outbursts and newspaper headlines – when he complained of being cold in one of the club's restaurant-bars and was told that the air-conditioning had not been regulated properly. On the way back to his office, he made a point of making a detour to the boiler-room to confront the person responsible.

'People who say I don't suffer fools gladly are wrong,' he says. 'I don't suffer fools at all.' Typical of this is a conversation – which he related during our meeting – concerning a TV researcher asking him to appear in a Channel Four interview with a 13-year-old girl who had complained about paying adult prices at Chelsea without getting adult privileges. 'I rang up this woman and asked who this girl supported. She said: "I don't know. She's on holiday." I said: "Oh, well what you have said in your fax isn't true. Fifteen per cent of our capacity is available for children." She said: "What about the other 85 per cent?" I then asked her what percentage of children did she think went to football matches and she replied that she didn't know. "So you want me to appear in a TV programme, with you and a 13-year-old girl who hasn't got her facts straight? Do me a favour – you're wasting my time." I suppose I am now the rude, arrogant Ken Bates as far as she is concerned, but half these people don't know what they're talking about.'

It seems a pity that Bates can provoke such negative feelings towards himself. West Ham's chief executive, Peter Storrie, often in Bates's company at Premiership club meetings, says: 'He comes up with some great ideas.' Indeed, Bates has long been a prominent figure on the various committees responsible for pushing English football as a whole in the right direction. The power he exudes is certainly respected by his fellow Premiership chairmen; in the election to represent the Premiership on the FA Council, he picked up 19 of the 20 votes. Moreover, while some players have voiced mixed feelings about him, many others speak highly of him. Gordon Taylor talks glowingly of Bates's spirit of generosity towards the former Chelsea centre-half Paul Elliott, when Elliott's career was shattered by a knee injury. 'Chelsea, who had him covered for what they had paid Celtic for him, were prepared to give him a good third of that, on top of other benefits to which he was legally entitled, plus a testimonial match.'

Still, it is par for the course for Bates that when you ask him to name his favourite Chelsea star he immediately plumps for David Speedie, one of the most fiery and aggressive of British post-war players and among those with the most unenviable disciplinary records. The Scottish international striker, who played for Chelsea from 1982 to 1988, clashed with his own team-mates as well as opponents. The most famous of his in-house Chelsea dust-ups was when he and his fellow Stamford Bridge striker Kerry Dixon had a heated argument in the dressing-room after a match and ended up throwing punches at each other. Speedie was at his most effective when he was fired up, so Bates has always looked upon him as a kindred spirit. 'The way Speedie played was the way I played. He was a winner. He would never take no for an answer on or off the field. He was so argumentative. I mean, he would have a row in the dressing-room with anybody. [Chelsea midfielder Nigel] Spackman would wind him up deliberately before a match and at 3 p.m. Speedie would be ready to kick the shit out of everybody on the field, fight for every ball. Then, at the end of the match, he'd come back into the dressing-room, go up to Spackman and pick up the argument from where they had left it before the game.

'I was at a Player of the Year function last season and I was chatting away when someone came up behind me and put his hands over my eyes. I just said: "Get them off, you little shit." I did not have to turn around to know it was Speedie. Only he would have done that.'

Bates was mainly responsible for signing the Scottish international. 'Before I left Wigan, we went up to Darlington, who had gone 21 matches unbeaten. We lost 3–1, and Speedie, who sat just in front of the Darlington back four, was the one who played the biggest part in it. He smashed up every one of our attacks *and* scored two goals. The other reason I remember it is that Darlington were going bust, and after the match, their chairman comes in and says: "Here you are, Mr Bates – we are doing a £1 draw, and you'll have a go, won't you? You're a rich man." He thought I was taking the mickey, because I gave him a £50 note. I don't think he'd ever seen one before. Anyway, when I got to Chelsea, I said to John Neal [the manager]: "Why don't we go and get Speedie?" John went to watch him a few times, and said: "I fancy him, chairman." So I went back to Darlington, went into the chairman's little office and signed him for £65,000. Speedie is still my favourite player in many ways. He was loyal. He would fight to the death for you.'

Bates's support for Speedie once put him in danger of being censured by the Football Association. Speedie was with Coventry City then, and Bates recalls: 'He actually agreed to cancel a family holiday he had booked to play in someone's testimonial match at Stamford Bridge.' During the game, every time he made a mistake, the crowd in the Shed (Chelsea's terrace area) howled and jeered at him and, typical of Speedie, he responded by dropping his shorts. A photographer from a freelance agency sold the picture to a newspaper, they printed it and Speedie was fined £750 by the FA. This so incensed Bates that he banned the agency from Stamford Bridge, and when Chelsea played Coventry the following season, he presented Speedie with a cheque for £750 on the pitch. 'Seven hundred and fifty quid – and a pair of shorts,' he recalls. 'Lord Justice Taylor criticised me for doing this when he wrote his report [on crowd problems in English football in general and the Hillsborough disaster in particular], but my reaction was that if this was all he had to moan about, there couldn't be much wrong with English football.'

The Speedie years at Chelsea were good years for Bates. He got on well with the manager, John Neal – 'The more I got to know him, the more I liked him' – and he clearly enjoyed the challenge of getting Chelsea back on their feet on the field as well as off it. Chelsea were in the Second Division when Bates took over; just two years later they were back in the First. 'We let seven players go on free transfers in the first year, John and I,' Bates says. 'I urged him to get on with it, do what he wanted. I was always saying to him: "What about this player, John? What about that player?" According to his assistant, Ian McNeill, I got him buzzing because before I arrived, the attitude had been "You can't do this" and "You can't do that".'

Bates's favourite anecdote about the quiet, introverted Neal concerns the signing of Nigel Spackman, like Speedie another bargain buy. 'Wigan owed me some money, which they couldn't repay, so Freddie Pye [the chairman] said to me: "Look, to wipe out the debt, take any player you want from us." So John and I went up to see a midweek match between Wigan and Bournemouth, and every 15 minutes Freddie is asking me: "Who do you fancy?" Five minutes before the end I turned to John and said: "Well, John, who do you fancy?" He says: "That number six looks good – the number six from Bournemouth." So we got Spackman for £45,000.'

Bates can get surprisingly sentimental over those days. At moments like this, and when he is scoring wisecrack points off you, it is difficult to believe that this is the man whose solution to the problem of supporters running on to Stamford Bridge pitch was to erect electric fences around it. It is interesting that the electricity was never turned on; it would seem to support the theory that Bates just likes to cause a stir and that his bark is much worse than his bite.

Still, when it comes to chairmen with intimidating images, he must be at the top of the list – along with Ellis and Sugar, of course.

SIX

Fan Power

R oy Blower, the proprietor of a Norwich roofing company, is a pleasant, affable man; the sort of football supporter whose loyalty to his club and sense of decency represent the lifeblood of British professional football.

But in the 1995–96 season Blower, in his capacity as the leader of Norwich City's Independent Supporters Association, was also a fan who could be described as every chairman's worst nightmare. He certainly came into that category in the case of Norwich's overlord Robert Chase, whose decision to sell his controlling interest in the club to the former chairman Geoffrey Watling at the end of the season stemmed in no small measure from the campaign that Blower had relentlessly generated against him and his controversial methods over a period of some eight years.

Just as all managers must expect to get the sack at some time, all chairmen appreciate the inevitability of their being haunted by a figure such as Blower.

You only have to attend the AGM of a Premiership or Football League club, especially when things are not going well for them, to appreciate how even normally mild-mannered supporters can sudden-ly be transformed into the most aggressive and cunning of interrogators. All chairmen have their favourite anecdotes of crossing swords with such followers. The chairman of one major club best remembers the moment when an overweight middle-aged woman stood up and protested that the season-ticket-holders' seats were not big enough. As the chairman was politely explaining the technical reasons why this problem could not be overcome, the director sitting next to him put an extra strain on his attempts to keep a straight face by muttering: 'With a bum like yours, we'd have to cut a row of seats by half.'

But sometimes such confrontations are no laughing matter, especially when the fans are venting their anger and frustration through match demonstrations necessitating police intervention.

'When the team are doing well, the managers and the players are wonderful; but when they are not, the chairman is awful,' said Leicester's Martin George. Hell, indeed, hath no fury like that of an avid football fan whose expectations have not been fulfilled. George experienced the whole gamut of the fans' emotions in 1995–96, with the supporters conducting a series of vehement protests against him, the board and manager Martin O'Neill, but ending up applauding them as a result of a remarkable late run which took Leicester into the promotion play-off competition and, ultimately, a dramatic 2–1 victory over Palace in the final at Wembley.

But the scale of the bitterness that had been directed at Martin George was lukewarm in comparison with that which the late Manchester City chairman Peter Swales had to endure before being forced to wave the white flag and sell out to Francis Lee's consortium in 1994. Not that this should be held against him. The wonder of Swales's contentious reign at Maine Road – stretching back 21 years, from October 1973 – was that he did not capitulate earlier. At the root of the fans' anger towards him was City's failure to escape the shadow of their neighbours at Old Trafford.

City had been one of the outstanding teams of the 1960s, and even though they had started to wane by the time Swales took over, his aim of keeping them in the same bracket as their arch rivals – the biggest club in Britain, let alone Manchester – did not look unreasonable.

If anybody caused Swales to believe that his reign would produce countless golden memories, it was Denis Law. Thirteen years earlier, when playing for United against City, Law had helped push the latter into the Second Division – and ensured his own team remained in the First – through gaining a decisive penalty. In 1974, a few months after Swales took the Maine Road chair, Law – by now a City player – repaid the debt by scoring the goal against his old club that sent them down to the Second Division. However, the expectations of a great future for City turned out to be an illusion.

The only trophy City ever won under Swales's chairmanship was the League Cup in 1976, and the picture of Swales as a man hopelessly ill-equipped for the task was underlined by the fact that he had no fewer than 12 managers, 11 of whom he sacked (eat your heart out, Messrs Ellis and Bates). Like Ellis, Swales was often labelled an egotist, and was one of Tommy Docherty's favourite wisecrack targets. (Peter Swales walks around with a sign around his neck which says: 'In the event of an accident, please call a press conference.') But, like Ellis, Swales, the chairman of the FA's International Committee, was also a man with an ultra-thick skin – although he had his breaking point like anyone else. The abuse that was heaped upon him after Manchester United won the Championship in 1993, for the first time in 26 years, was too much even for him to bear. It was bad enough that Swales was subjected to demonstrations against him at City's Maine Road matches, and that damage was done to his radio and TV shop in Altrincham. He and his family were also intimidated at their home – he had to have armed guards outside for a number of weeks – and some fans even tried to confront his 87-year-old mother in her private nursing home. Under this sort of pressure, Swales, an unprepossessing figure, became more haunted by the week.

After he had relinquished control at Maine Road, and right up to his death in 1996, I was the only journalist to be granted a full interview with him, even though I had never previously met him. It was perhaps inevitable that Swales, having seen his high-profile misjudgements rebounding on him so heavily, should wish to drift out of the limelight. It was perhaps also typical of the man that he should look upon being featured in a book about chairmen as less of a threat to his exile from the mainstream of top professional football than appearing in a newspaper or TV programme. It was fortunate for me. The insights Swales provided into what lurks behind the glamour of a chairman's position were poignant to say the least, as was his appraisal of himself.

'I should have realised that my time was up long before I did – probably two years before, or when we lost to Spurs in the Cup [the sixth round of the FA Cup in 1993, when City fans invaded the pitch to try and get the tie abandoned]. I should have had someone else in the chair, and sat back as a director. But I had been in the chair for almost 20 years, and I had it in my mind to be the first to do the 20, you see.

'Even when United won the Championship, I felt I had time to ease myself out of things. I knew the City fans would be upset about United's success, but I don't think I quite grasped the extent of it and what it would mean for me. For years, when a United supporter wound up a City supporter by pointing out that we'd been relegated, or that they had won the Cup, the City fan could always turn around and say: "So what – you still haven't won the Championship." Then, United win the title and all of a sudden, Francis Lee appears on the scene and obviously the City supporters react to him – it's dead simple, really.

'I had already interviewed several prominent people [to take over the chairmanship] who could have done an excellent job, and then as soon as all the trouble started, they backed off – they didn't like what they were seeing. As for myself, the supporters were dead against me and most of my own directors were dead against me. My attitude was: "Okay, they [the Lee consortium] are going to take the club over, but they are going to have to pay for it." That's fair enough, isn't it? If you want to buy something, you have to pay for it. But it became a long-drawn-out battle, and really, when I look back on it now, I think: "Bloody hell, how did you manage to keep it going for six months?"

'The ironic thing about it was that for nearly 20 years I had probably put myself out more than anybody else to establish a rapport with the supporters. I had travelled all over the country and even to Scotland, Wales and Ireland, to attend functions. I remember a big City Supporters Club rally in Manchester in the early '70s, when they gave me this fantastic standing ovation – it was one of the highlights of my years at the club. In fact, I felt more comfortable mixing with the supporters than I was with the City players. I was a washout when it came to being close to the players; I probably had a few hang-ups about them, in that deep down I thought they got paid too much money and did too little work. With the supporters, it was different. Only last week, I went to this golfing dinner. Francis Lee was at the next table, and when the bloke who had won the competition was presented with the trophy, he stood up and said: "Oh, it's nice to see the past and present City chairmen here, and I would like to present this cup to them so that they can put it in the Maine Road trophy room." It brought the bloody house down – it was the sort of thing that people associated with City got all the time. But most of it was said and taken in good spirit, so it was difficult for me to come to terms with some of the things that happened to me.

'I could cope with the demonstrations by City fans at the ground, but the more sinister stuff was something else. For me, the people who really made the whole thing so hard for me were not the true City fans, but hooligans who just latched on to the situation just for the sake of causing bother. It was when I started feeling threatened at my home that it started getting desperate for me. "I'm in real trouble here," I thought. I came home one night and there was a bloke in the garage. I got followed home several times – Jean and the children [his wife and three daughters] were also followed. Then there were the threatening phone calls. They were the worst. We had to change our number three times. I think the worst day was when I had two or three phone calls at work to say: "Just remember that we know where your mother is." Two lads actually went into the nursing home – there was no violence, but they actually walked into the place, presented themselves to her and walked out again. It was shocking. They were more or less telling me what they could do, what could happen.

'My wife was frightened to death, the children were frightened to death, and I was scared, too – well, frightened to death, really.'

Swales was equally frank – disconcertingly so – about the mistakes that led to his nightmare. 'I was obsessed with trying to catch up with United. When I look back on it, I can see that City will possibly never be as big as United. I realise that now. But at the time, well, there's nothing wrong in making an effort, is there? In the earlier part of my chairmanship especially, I think I would have been a pretty rough ride for the people who worked with me. In my determination to catch up with United, I went a bit potty. I started making mistakes and I made bad mistakes.'

In the main, these concerned his managers. 'I do feel sorry for chairmen sometimes because they can't always tell the truth,' he said. 'When you sack a manager, it is not always politic to explain exactly why you sacked him. And most chairmen panic, don't they?' This, he says, was the trap he fell into when he sacked Ron Saunders, after Saunders – who had only been at Maine Road for five months – had taken City to the 1974 League Cup final (which they lost 2–1 to Wolves). Swales admits that he was too influenced by the criticism that some of City's senior stars – among them Lee and Mike Summerbee – levelled at Saunders. 'Some people in that team, who were getting near the end of their careers, didn't like Ron because he was a tough disciplinarian and they didn't think he showed them enough respect. He'd refer to Lee as "Fatty", things like that. He had a way of saying things to them that upset them. I am not sure that the decision to sack him was totally wrong, but that was the last time I allowed myself to be influenced by players.'

Even more embarrassing to him was the memory of his bringing Malcolm Allison back to City as team manager at the expense of Tony Book, whose five years in the job had won City the League Cup in 1976, the runners-up spot in the First Division in 1977 and excellent signings such as Asa Hartford, Joe Royle, Dave Watson,

Brian Kidd and Mike Channon. 'We were at last on the brink of catching United. The season we finished runners-up to Liverpool in the Championship, there is no doubt that we would have won the title but for the injury to Colin Bell, and we had got our average gate to within 2,000 to 3,000 of United's average gate. I tell you, they were doing no good at the time, and we were doing quite well. But we messed it up and it was my fault. You know, my logic was that, having done well with a fellow [Book] who is not the best manager in the world, if we got someone better, we were bound to win it. It's a mistake you can easily make, isn't it? I'd like to be able to go back and do what I should have done. But I've got to remember that period as it was and think about some of the constructive things I did.'

Swales remained a City shareholder after his departure as chairman, but put some distance between himself and the new board, even with the members of it with whom he had worked. 'They don't really talk to me,' he said. 'I suppose it would be like conversing with the enemy camp to them. It's a shame, of course, but I wouldn't dream of embarrassing them by ringing them up and saying what about a spot of lunch or dinner or can we go out together? They have to be seen to be showing loyalty to the new bosses, which is fair enough.'

However, Swales did spend more time with other clubs, and other directors, and he did see what lies on the other side of that role for his counterparts of today. 'If you run an ordinary business, it's usually quiet — you just concentrate on making a profit and developing the company and people know very little about you. Now, anybody connected with one of the major clubs can hardly step off the pavement without everybody knowing about it.

'This business of being the chairman of a major club has become more and more a young man's game. The pressure has become incredible. I was in my early 40s when I started as City's chairman, and life was a ball then because I was so full of energy. But once I started getting towards my late 50s, it became a strain. I can't visualise any of the relatively new Premiership chairmen lasting 20 years. The job eventually wears you down; you become punch drunk. This has always been the case, but more so now than ever, I would say.

'People like me are going to be in and out of football like yo-yos in the next few years,' he added. 'Unless you've got the money of Alan Sugar, Peter Johnson or Sir John Hall, it is going to be very difficult for a chairman to survive at the top level. The supporters will sort you out eventually; they'll soon know if you haven't got the cash to get them the best players and they'll get rid of you. I might have been the first or the second or the third, but I won't be the last, that's for sure.'

When he said that, in the summer of 1995, Norwich had been relegated from the Premiership and Robert Chase, a chairman as single-minded in the face of criticism as Swales had been, was about to start what proved the last round in his battle with the Norwich fans in general and Roy Blower in particular.

For much of the season, Blower, the initiator of a fans' boycott of Norwich's home matches, was showing signs of frustration, if not desperation. To Blower and many other supporters, Chase had consistently put his business head before his football heart, and concentrated on building up the club's capital assets at the expense of the team.

It is a claim that has been made of other chairmen, of course, but Chase was regarded as taking this approach to the game too far. It says much about the force of Blower's campaign against the chairman's methods that, with Norwich looking in danger of being relegated again (after the departure of their new manager, Martin O'Neill, to Leicester following a bust-up with Chase) that his name was mentioned almost as much in the local newspapers and radio and television as the team.

But the harder Blower and his troops pushed for the resignation of Chase, the more determined the chairman stood his ground. It was an intriguing spectacle, not least because of Blower's assertion that Chase had become paranoid enough about his safety to hire bodyguards to accompany him to and from the ground and to avoid watching Norwich's home matches from the directors' box or any other spots from which he could be easily seen and reached by spectators. Not surprisingly, both claims were denied by Chase's PR department. 'He has always tended to prefer to watch matches on the TV in places like the sponsors' lounge or the police control room,' one spokesman insisted. 'The reason is simply that he feels it necessary to see as much of our match-day operation as he can, so that any problems can be eradicated and he can keep developing [the way things are done].' Nevertheless it was difficult to avoid thinking of Chase as a man on the run, and of Blower as the man who would never stop pursuing him.

Blower's energy in that department – his campaigning zeal – is very much a family trait. He says that the characteristic has been inherited from his grandfather, a leading light in the long, bitter national agricultural strike of the 1920s, and his father, a trade unionist and ETU member for 40 years. It has led to a succession of Blower-inspired local community initiatives, such as the raising of money to provide or improve leisure and recreational facilities. But it is his long battle with Chase, full of political thrusts and counter thrusts, which clearly absorbed him the most.

Six years younger than Chase at 53, Blower has been a Norwich fan since the age of five, and for 37 years did all manner of voluntary jobs for the club. He started selling raffle tickets at 12, and eventually ended up as the co-ordinator of the fans' forum. This role, which he filled for six and a half years, until March 1993, made him virtually a Norwich supporters' ombudsman. 'A football club should be a caring club' was his motto, as he threw himself into responsibilities such as organising the presentation of tankards to the oldest Norwich fans, and trying to ensure that all the Carrow Road faithful's needs were being catered for. Chase himself acknowledged Blower's commitment to Norwich when he wrote him a letter stating that he was a 'fantastic servant' of the club.

However, as the supporters' needs included a successful football team as well as that of a well-appointed stadium, the temptation to keep questioning the chairman's methods – a Blower preoccupation which had effectively started with the controversial Chase sackings of Norwich's popular manager, Ken Brown, and the club secretary, Nigel Pleasance, in 1987 – became increasingly difficult to resist. 'The fact that I was employed by the club did not mean they could gag me,' Blower explained.

One of his numerous gripes with Chase concerned ticket prices. 'When Carrow Road was converted into an all-seater stadium, Mr Chase said that he would operate a transitional policy with regards to the increase in ticket prices. After just one season, he hiked them up by more than 66 per cent. I don't call that a transitional policy. When the press interviewed me, I had to be honest and say that I felt he had kicked the supporters in the teeth.'

Ironically, according to Blower, it was not Chase who relieved him of his position at the club, but another member of the board 'because he felt I had become slightly bigger than the directors'. Moreover, Blower does not blame Chase for the fact that although the chairman encouraged him to apply for the full-time post of community officer at Carrow Road a few years ago, he did not even make the shortlist. But it was Chase who continued to be Blower's number-one target.

In some ways, the conflict between the two men, which prompted an avalanche of 'Chase Must Go' coffee mugs and 'Let Him Know it's Time to Go' badges, had a strangely civilised undertone, with the pair clearly intent on keeping their emotions in check. Blower felt this was essential in dealing with someone as 'politically clever' as Chase.

Politically? One of Chase's favourite anecdotes concerns the early part of his spell as Norwich chairman, when he deemed it important to get on to the Football League Management Committee so that he could 'know what was going on in the inner circle of the game'. There was one place up for grabs, and both he and Bobby Charlton were in contention for it. In view of Charlton's immense stature in the game, it seemed a case of 'no contest'. But Chase recalls: 'All the chairmen and secretaries in the League were there and Bobby Charlton said he would address the meeting first. Fine. I knew enough to appreciate that the best strategy was to be very humble and very brief. But Bobby took the opportunity to tell them what he would do for football and he went on and on. The more he did so, the more I began to think that my chances were better than I had expected. When it was my turn, I just said: "Gentlemen, I don't want to hold you up any longer because you have a programme to keep to. If I was elected, I would simply do my very best to carry out your wishes. Thank you for listening to me." I won by two votes.'

'A great politician,' Blower said. 'I had loads of personal meetings with him, and found that he would tell you something one day, and then the complete opposite the next day.'

It is a claim that Chase has had some difficulty brushing aside after selling Chris Sutton to Blackburn in the summer of 1994, not long after proclaiming: 'I can assure supporters that if Chris Sutton is not at Carrow Road at the start of next season, I won't be here either.' In truth, Chase has possibly been criticised over that more than he deserved. Situations can change dramatically in football and Norwich's manager at the time, John Deehan, mindful that the player was determined to leave, put some pressure on Chase to sell him sooner rather than later so that he and the team could work in their pre-season training on ways to compensate for his loss. Chase's statement, however, was something which, with the help of Blower, the chairman was never allowed to forget.

Typical of the relationship between the two was their conversation following a local newspaper interview with Blower in December 1995. That night, Chase telephoned him at home and, without raising his voice, said: 'I have just been reading that you are calling for my resignation. I just want to say, Roy, that I am deeply offended.'

'Well, chairman, you keep putting the blame for things [Norwich's indifferent results] on the football department,' Blower told him, equally calmly. 'But, with the greatest respect, it's like the captain of the ship blaming the first mate.'

'Well, if that's the case,' Chase replied, still cool, calm and collected, 'our dialogue is broken, Roy.' With that he hung up.

On another occasion, when Chase mistakenly got a fact wrong about an obscure Norwich match when the club were in the old Third Division (South) – while trying to explain to Blower that his expectations were unreasonably high – his adversary was onto it in a flash: 'Chairman, you don't know the history of your own club.'

Blower refutes the suggestion that his campaign to drive Chase out became an obsession: 'I don't think it was ever an obsession. When it is an obsession, I think you are inclined to lose sight of what you are aiming at.' He paused, and thought of a better way to put it. 'Somebody actually wrote from Kansas to say that Roy Blower had mounted a crusade. The dictionary definition of that word is that it is an aggressive force against an evil power.' He accepts that the latter description, in its literal sense, could hardly be applied to Chase. But football pride and passion can know no bounds, even in a place like Norfolk; and Blower, going through every Chase statement and decision with a fine tooth-comb, was not willing to let the chairman get away with anything.

'Mr Chase said that it was unreasonable to expect Norwich to be a leading Premiership club because the city has a population of only 120,000. That was a perfect example of how he used facts and figures to back up his arguments and pull the wool over your eyes. The point he was making was an affront to our fans, many of whom come from rural areas. Norfolk has a population of more than 600,000 and the closest clubs to Norwich are Ipswich, 45 miles away in one direction, and Peterborough, 80 miles away in another.'

It was the sort of rhetoric to which Chase became accustomed. The obvious question is – why?

Norwich City started the week of 10 March 1996 languishing in the middle of the Endsleigh League First Division, with the three other teams relegated from the Premiership the previous season looking down on them.

While it certainly seemed unlikely that Norwich could climb back to the top level at their first attempt, it was by no means out of the question, however. There were still 11 matches to go, and the team were only ten points behind the side in the fourth and final promotion play-off spot. English football contains many examples of the sort of sudden inspired run that Norwich needed to get into that position.

But Robert Chase then emphasised once again that he is nothing if not a pragmatist. Norwich were between £4 million and £5 million in debt, largely because of ground improvements undertaken with short-term loans; and Chase was not about to let his heart rule his head and wait to see if Norwich could regain their financial balance through their results on the field. That week, he sold Norwich's captain Jon Newsome to Sheffield Wednesday for £1.6 million while their leading scorer Ashley Ward went to Derby for £1 million.

From the outside, this was seen as a remarkable move, even by the standards of a man who had sold more than £27 million worth of players during his nine years at the helm, but spent no more than half of that sum on replacing them; a man who had long invited speculation that he was only truly interested in building up the club's capital assets so that Norwich could be floated on the Stock Exchange and he could then sell his shares at a massive profit.

It was a move that also reflected Chase's courage. He was already in more than enough trouble with the Norwich fans. In December, Martin O'Neill, whom he had appointed as the new team manager the previous summer in succession to John Deehan, had walked out on the club to join Leicester, claiming that he had not been given as much money to improve the team as he had expected. Even before the sales of Newsome and Ward, Norwich fans had delivered a 10,000-signature petition demanding Chase's resignation; and the player sales were sandwiched between an EGM to try and force the chairman out on a shareholders' vote and the club's AGM. In the midst of all this, he had Blower keeping up his propaganda war with information such as Norwich falling more than £4 million into the red; having a loan of £2.1 million and a bank overdraft of £2.4

million, which were costing £10,000 a week to service; and losing £60,000 a match in gate receipts through a 6,000 drop in the club's average home attendance.

So, not for the first time, Robert Chase showed that whatever he might have lacked as a football club chairman, it wasn't balls.

Chase, whom I interviewed in the summer of 1995, had always clung to the belief that it was essential for clubs to be run on proper business principles, to be realistic about their capabilities and true place in the game's financial pecking order, and not be tempted to spend money they couldn't afford. 'Clubs no longer compete against each other on a level field,' he said, referring to the manner in which relatively small, unfashionable clubs like Norwich have been affected by the abolition of the players' maximum wage, the success players have gained in their freedom-of-contract campaigns and the end of clubs sharing gate receipts. 'I am not criticising these changes – I realise they had to take place – but I don't think it was fully appreciated how much the original concept of the league would be changed as a result. That concept, of clubs competing against each other on equal terms, has been lost. You take the change in gate receipts. At one time, it didn't matter if you had a bigger ground and attracted more spectators than I did. When you played at my place, you took half of my £20,000 and when I played at your place, I took half of your £100,000. The money was distributed evenly. Again, I am not complaining about this; all I'm saying is that clubs like ours have to be aware of our limitations and be practical.'

Chase is not the only chairman who has made this point. Even in the top flight, clubs outside the select group of big-city giants like Manchester United, Liverpool, Newcastle and Arsenal, have become neurotic about the dangers of trying to take on these clubs at their own big-spending game.

Some of the most vivid examples can be found in London, at Wimbledon and Crystal Palace. Wimbledon, the smallest crowd-pullers in the Premiership, and the only club without their own ground to boost their income in other areas, are to Manchester United what a small corner shop is to Sainsbury's. Their Lebanese owner, Sam Hammam, runs the tightest financial ship at this level, repeatedly avoiding a financial crash on the rocks by buying players cheaply and making a profit on them through transfers to better-off rivals. In the circumstances, Wimbledon have done wonders to last as long as they have at the top level, a tribute to the virtues of motivation, hard work and the willingness of their managers to attempt to perfect the art of building bricks without straw. Another surprising aspect of Wimbledon's success story is that despite the taste of glamour occasionally experienced by their fans – particularly when Wimbledon beat Liverpool in the 1988 FA Cup final – they have remained philosophical about the structure and methods which have prevented the club giving them more.

Ron Noades, Hammam's predecessor at Wimbledon, got his hands on a club with far greater potential in Crystal Palace. Nonetheless, the basic principles on which he now runs Palace, especially with regard to their transfer-market and wages policies, are quite similar. When Noades discusses the need for clubs to avoid taking rash financial chances, and the importance of not putting the cart of players before the horse of developing their grounds, it is strangely reminiscent of Chase's philosophy.

As with Norwich under Chase, Palace have had a chequered life under Noades, relegated three times and promoted twice. The view that their success has been achieved in spite of his methods, rather than because of them, appeared to be particularly valid in the 1995–96 season. Having sold virtually all the club's most highly rated 1994–95 players, and spent little more than a third of that income on replacements, the team looked in the same state of disarray as Norwich at one stage. But Palace did reach the First Division's promotion play-off final while Norwich finished in the bottom half of the table, thus leaving Chase a bigger target for public dissatisfaction than ever. But it did little to shake his belief that his cautious, hard-headed business approach to football, while widely condemned as being far too extreme, was right.

Born and raised in the Norfolk fishing village of Caister, Chase, whose father worked in the construction industry, was never one to address himself to the more idealistic or philosophical side of life. Unlike his two brothers, he did not shine academically ('I was always in the bottom three in my class') but he did show his worth in entrepreneurial ventures such as selling the teachers at his school the eggs from the chickens he looked after. Like so many chairmen, he went on to strike it rich in the building and property-development business. 'I saw an opportunity and grabbed it with both hands. I remember buying my first piece of land. I borrowed £1,000 and my mother said to me: "Whatever do you think you are doing? It's going to get totally out of control." But, you know, I paid it off in six months and I said to my mother: "There you are – I'm going to do it again, and this time I'm borrowing £10,000."'

Although Chase says he has been a Norwich City supporter since the age of seven, when his father first took him to Carrow Road, seeing an opportunity and grabbing it with both hands could also be one way of summing up why he took over the club in 1985. He was well known to the club's directors through his company's ownership of one of the first Carrow Road executive boxes, and their sponsorship of Norwich's youth teams. 'It's very simple,' he recalled. 'Norwich were in big financial trouble, and one morning I got a call from Sir Arthur Smout [the chairman] asking if I could make the club a loan. I told him, no, I wouldn't do that but I'd buy some shares. I actually bought 25,000 £1 shares, that at the time had a market value of one pence each. The business had no assets – no net assets – and was struggling to go on from day to day. We completed the purchase of the shares by 3.30 p.m. that day – I later found out that the board needed the deal to be done at that speed because of their situation at the bank.' His wife, he said, thought he had gone 'crazy'. But Chase's finely tuned instincts told him differently: 'I saw it as a grand opportunity. I thought that Norwich had just lost their way a little bit and that we could reorganise it. They had some great assets – I mean, I saw a seven-acre freehold site in the centre of Norwich as being a terrific asset.'

To Chase, the financial mess he inherited stemmed from the determination of Sir Arthur South to push Norwich to the top, no matter what the price. The partnership of South and his similarly bold, ambitious manager, John Bond, was nothing if not exciting to the fans. But Chase, while readily praising the work of these two men in putting Norwich firmly on the big-time football map, has mixed feelings about the degree of self-indulgence in terms of what was paid in players' transfer fees and wages, and the general organisation of the club. 'Sir Andrew threw caution to the wind in getting Norwich from the Third Division South to the First,' Chase said. 'The criticism levelled at me is that I have gone too much the other way. But we have to spend £1 million a month, or there-abouts, and if you don't run it like a business – and don't have a personal fortune to dip into to keep topping it up – you'll soon run into problems. At my first board meeting, I was asking how much different players were earning, what contracts they were on, and quite clearly no one had any idea.'

Chase's first steps were to bring a greater sense of order and teamwork to the club by assessing what Norwich were capable of achieving – with the help of a firm of market consultants – and giving all the members of staff a more precise breakdown of their individual responsibilities so as to enable them to complement each other. 'They all had one principal objective, which was to work with Norwich FC and to win. But it was a bit like village football, and I don't mean that disrespectfully. They were all running where the ball went, and all you were doing was exhausting yourself and leaving gaps elsewhere. It's a bit like flying an aircraft – the pilot is the most important man, but he needs a huge team to get that plane off the ground. They can't all be sitting behind the controls.'

That argument seems reasonable enough. So does Chase's explanation of why, after Norwich's relegation to the Second Division in the year he became chairman, he sold the two players – centre-half Dave Watson (to Everton) and goalkeeper Chris Woods (to Rangers) – who had played starring roles in their League Cup triumph that same year and whom many considered vital to the club's chances of being promoted again. 'To get out of the financial muddle we were in, the selling of those players was one of two alternatives. The other was to sell the freehold of the ground and rent it back. We got £1.75 million for Watson and Woods and it was as if all our Christmases had come at once. We were able to pay our debts. We were able to get our heads above water.' Moreover, that season Norwich also gained promotion back to the First Division.

But two seasons later, Chase's approach really did start to raise alarm bells among Norwich fans. Though the team made a poor start to the season, it still came as a shock when Chase sacked Ken Brown, one of the most popular figures in the game and arguably the most successful manager in Norwich's history. Brown was axed in November 1987, almost seven years to the day that he took over from John Bond after a long spell as Bond's assistant. While stressing that this was one of the most difficult decisions he has ever had to make, Chase maintains that Brown owed much to his assistant, Mel Machin, who complemented him perfectly, and lost much of his effectiveness when Machin left for Manchester City. Chase told me: 'If you have a production line, with two managers on it, one is the front man who walks down in his smart suit, the man who says good morning to everybody and who everybody wants to talk to, and the other is the one with the oil and a rag, the one who kicks backsides and makes things buzz. With Ken Brown and Mel Machin, we had exactly that. It was suggested by your fellow journalists, in the nicest possible way, that Mel Machin was really the influence in the success we were enjoying while Ken Brown was manager. When Mel Machin left, I think Ken Brown wanted to disprove that view but, in actual fact, your colleagues were proved right.'

Chase claimed that he finally decided that Brown had to go when he overheard a conversation between the manager and Steve Bruce, then Norwich's centre-half and captain. 'We'd had a bad result and, from the top of the stairs, I happened to overhear Ken telling Steve to get the lads together so they could all watch a video of the match and put things right, and Bruce shouting something to the effect that he [Brown] still wouldn't be able to put his finger on the problems.

'The manager had lost his way,' Chase maintained. 'Sadly, that happens in every business.'

Chase puts up a similar case in defence of his decision to part company with Deehan following Norwich's relegation from the Premiership in 1995 after just one season with Deehan in charge. There was considerable sympathy for Deehan when he took the job, not least because of the view that when a club offload as many good players as Norwich have done, it is bound to catch up with them at some time, no matter who the manager might be. In Deehan's case, losing Chris Sutton to Blackburn was part of a 1994 Norwich sales period which also included the transfers of other exciting front players such as Ruel Fox to Newcastle and Efan Ekoku to Wimbledon. But this point seemed to be lost on Chase, who prefers to hit you with the fact that such problems were not borne out by a good start to the season that earned Norwich seventh place in the table by the end of December. 'I don't think it was inevitable that we would be relegated,' he retorted. 'I mean, I can knock that one on the head just by mentioning Coventry. Their attendance figures are similar to ours but I don't think they have ever been relegated, have they?' The obvious answer to that is that Coventry have not sold as many of their best players as Norwich have. But Chase, in reply to the observation that some managers are confronted by bigger problems than others, said: 'Every business has to contend with this. That's what good management is about – dealing with problems, getting over problems.'

He felt that the partnership between Deehan and his assistant Gary Megson (who subsequently became manager) did not work as well as it might have. 'I don't think anyone's ever had such a bad end to the season,' Chase said, referring to Norwich's record of only one win from their last 20 matches of 1994–95. 'It just shows you how volatile football can be. Sometimes the chemistry is right, sometimes it isn't.'

If you follow Chase's logic, he himself could be accused of below-par management then. He admitted: 'We did not think it was possible for us to be relegated, and we were just too patient with the whole set-up. We should have acted more quickly. I'm not saying we should have sacked John, but he did need help. At some time or another, the chairman has to say to the manager: "What are you going to do? Something needs to happen." I don't think the transfers of players like Chris Sutton created our problem. I just think we got it wrong and were slow dealing with it. Remember, John Deehan did not have a lot of experience in managing and I think the whole situation put an immense strain on him. He had lost weight – I mean, you only had to look at him to know he wasn't enjoying it. I would not dream of knocking him because he is an excellent coach and did a superb job for us until the going got tough. When we started losing, there was a need for a strong, positive and clear sense of direction, and we were too slow in asking questions such as: "Does John need a break from it? Has he got too uptight and confused?"'

Mike Walker also came up through the ranks of the Carrow Road coaching staff to take on the manager's job, from 1992 to 1994. In his first season, Norwich finished in their highest-ever league position – third in the Premiership – and in a rousing UEFA Cup run the following season, they belied their inexperience at this level by becoming the first English team to beat European giants Bayern Munich in Germany. However, as if to reinforce the impression of Chase as a man who takes the view that talented football professionals grow on trees, he allowed Walker to leave over a contractual dispute.

Of all the contentious decisions Chase made as Norwich chairman, this was the one that probably had the most adverse effect on his relationship with the fans. What made it particularly damaging to him was that the conflict between the two men was brought into the open publicly, with Walker's version of it merely rubber-stamping all the old misgivings about Chase's approach to the game.

Manchester United's Martin Edwards once confided to a colleague: 'The worst thing you can do is to get into a public dispute with the manager. When that happens, the chairman is always going to be the loser.' It is perhaps significant that when Alex Ferguson was negotiating a new contract with United in the summer of 1996, the matter was settled relatively quietly and seemingly amicably, even though, according to insiders, the club were staggered at the terms he had requested. Ferguson ended up with a contract reportedly worth £1 million a year.

But, of course, Norwich are not Manchester United, as Chase made a point of stressing when I broached the subject of Walker with him. He emphasised that it wasn't so much the duration of the contract that Walker was seeking that was the problem to him, but the amount of money it would have meant Norwich being forced to pay him if they ever decided to terminate it. 'Mike Walker could have had a 100-year contract here if he had wanted it, but what I couldn't afford was the clause that said I would have to pay up the remainder in full if things went wrong and we had to part company with him.'

He cited the case of Everton, who appointed Walker as their manager in 1994 and who became involved in a lengthy wrangle with him over compensation after sacking him later that year. Walker's predecessor at Goodison was Howard Kendall, and Chase says: 'He had a clause in his contract stating that if he left them at any time before the end of it he would have to pay them £150,000; and if he was dismissed, *they* would have to pay *him* £150,000. I would love to be in a position to offer a manager the sort of contract that Everton offered Mike Walker. Look at people like Peter Johnson and Jack Walker, who have sunk millions of pounds into their clubs. I admire what they have done, but we are not in that position here. In Norwich's entire history, the maximum amount of new capital pumped into the club has been £150,000 – that's what we are competing against.

'On average, the football club has made a £150,000 profit per season over the last ten years. So forget Mike Walker, forget the manager – we would not sign a contract with anyone where the penalty for getting out of the agreement was equivalent to three years' profit. What sound businessman would do that?'

Maybe, but in the light of Walker's fate, and that of the high number of players Norwich have sold, their level of ambition – at least in terms of football performances and results – has not appeared very high. Chase's attitude to this was that Norwich should not get ideas above their station but should, for the time being, be proud of their reputation as a star breeding-ground. 'Players come here because they see it as a wonderful career move; we've probably given more people the opportunity to move on for a million pounds than any other football club I can think of. If you're looking at a career structure for a journalist, he can't go into one of the posh papers and demand a column – he has to climb up the ladder. If I had a son in football, I would have thought that Norwich was a wonderful stepping-stone for him.

'You see, it's not always a question of "Shall we sell him?" but of "Can we keep him?". Take Andy Linighan [the former Norwich central defender]. He came from Oldham for £150,000 and £350 a week. Once Arsenal came in for him, there was no way you were going to keep him. Same with Robert Fleck and Andy Townsend. I don't think we could have kept any of them.'

Could Norwich not have done so by loosening their purse strings? Chase shook his head: 'We can't do three things at once. The first thing we had to do was get the finances right, and the second thing has been to get the stadium right. It has needed a lot of money spent on it, and we are nearly there now. I mean, the carpark, which we were renting, has cost us £1 million to buy; we've bought the land behind the south stand for £1 million; we've bought our training ground – I would not have wanted to miss any of these opportunities. On reflection, I think that over the last ten years, we've done most things right.'

Unfortunately for Chase, the Norwich public did not agree. They were particularly angered over his stance concerning Martin O'Neill. At the time of O'Neill's acrimonious departure, Chase told me that Norwich's relegation had left them with a wage bill of £3.8 million against gate receipts of £2.6 million. He added: 'When he came to Norwich, Martin was told quite clearly that we operated within a budget. We allowed him to bring in Matthew Rush, who got a bad injury on his first day here. That pushed the wage bill up by £150,000. Then we allowed him to sign Robert Fleck, which pushed the wage bill up by a similar amount. Then, when he wanted to bring in a third one, we had to say: "Look here, Martin, what we think you ought to do now is find a way to operate within your budget. If we give in to you, all the other departments will expect me to give them what they want, too. I will even have my secretary asking for a new chair."'

The final straw for O'Neill was Chase's refusal to agree to the signing of Dean Windass from Hull for £700,000, on the grounds that the striker was nearly 27 and would have affected the percentage of Norwich players with a potentially high resale value.

It was perhaps fortunate for Chase that he was no longer on the Carrow Road scene when O'Neill steered Leicester back into the Premiership, with the help of a goal from Steve Claridge, a much travelled 30-year-old striker whom he had been allowed to buy from Birmingham for more than £1 million. But then, having watched Chase under direct attack from Norwich's shareholders at the club's AGM the previous month, you are inclined to suggest that he suffered more than enough anyway.

On the day of my meeting with Chase, in the summer of 1995, Carrow Road was staging a Jehovah's Witness convention. On the next occasion, 21 March 1996, I saw him in a rather more highly charged environment – in the sponsors lounge, facing a barrage of searching questions, and abuse, at the club's AGM.

As I passed through the farming village of Wymondham on the way into Norwich, I saw a poster advertising a play by the local amateur drama society called *A Chorus of Disapproval*. The sounds of dissent were nothing compared to those that had been heard in and around Carrow Road over the previous 12 months, although this would have bothered Chase less than a lot of other people. Shortly after he sacked Ken Brown, a crate of empty milk bottles was thrown through the window of his Rolls-Royce, while he was sitting in it. 'We've had no end of security people employed – we've even had an explosive device sent to the club,' he said. 'My wife's a nervous wreck; she can't stand the criticism, but I am lucky enough to have a small flat in London and a small holiday home in Spain, and when things start to upset her, she packs up and moves out.' He shrugged and added: 'It doesn't upset me a bit. I'm used to it.'

Indeed, it is not just in football that Chase had become acclimatised to aggro. In addition to his position as chairman of the Norfolk police authority, he has also filled prominent positions on local health and education councils. 'Being chairman of a football club is tough, but it's no tougher than if you're trying to build a motorway or close a school or a hospital. I've had chairs thrown at me, I've had the sleeve pulled right out of my jacket – people do feel very passionately about things and sometimes they go over the top. But it's part and parcel of having a democracy, people being free to criticise. I don't mind that at all.'

His performance at Norwich's AGM emphasises this. Half an hour before the start, the Norwich employee at the front door confides: 'This is going to be interesting, but he [Chase] is good in these situations. He would fit in well at Westminster.' An elderly gentleman, the first shareholder to arrive, likens him to Margaret Thatcher: 'Did a good job for seven years, but then . . .' Once the action starts, in a room packed with some 200 mostly antagonistic shareholders, you quickly appreciate that he has a good point. Chase looks pale and drawn in the knowledge that this is going to be the most hostile of all the AGMs since he took over the club. He is on a platform with the other members of the board, and among those in the front row of the audience itching to give him a hard time are Ken Brown and, of course, his old adversary, Blower. Still, as the verbal blows against him intensify, you have to give him seven out of ten for his ability to keep his cool, albeit without looking particularly confident.

After a timid opening round, relating to the minutes of the previous AGM, the battle starts to warm up when Chase talks about his 'concern' that Norwich's 1996 bid for promotion has not succeeded – 'Why not?' cries a voice from the back of the room – and the club's determination to do better next time. 'I've said in the past, and I don't mind repeating it today, that if there is anybody with the intent and the resources to take over my job, I will not hesitate to stand aside,' he adds. He goes on to explain that one of the stumbling blocks to this is that prospective buyers of his shares had requested information about the club's finances that he was loath to provide, on the grounds that it might leave him vulnerable to a 'conflict of interests' charge. He asks the audience to consider the idea of giving prospective buyers the details they need through a specially commissioned report by a national independent firm of auditors.

'Are you saying that our own auditors are not capable of providing this information?' he is asked. 'And how much do you want for your shares? That's what everybody wants to know.'

Chase replies that he would welcome the exercise being carried out by Norwich's accountants. 'But I am only trying to be as fair as possible.' Then, referring to the second part of the question, he suddenly raises the opposition's adrenalin level by revealing: 'I *have* had an offer for my shares, one that *would* be acceptable to me, but they are unwilling to proceed until such time that this exercise is carried out.'

Enter a woman who fires the first real shot at him: 'The best thing you can do for this club is to step down and take your board – sychophants who are masquerading as a board – with you.'

Loud applause, and cries of 'Hear, Hear'.

'Take the money now while they [the shares] are worth something,' she says.

'We could be in the Second Division if you don't,' says someone else in support, 'and then you'll have even more egg on your face.'

Chase is unmoved. 'I have had an offer, which I am prepared to accept, but they are not prepared to go ahead until this process is gone through.'

The woman attacks again: 'I just want you to say that you will not turn around at the end of the day and say: "I have changed my mind because it's not in the best interests of the football club."'

'I have already said that I am prepared to sell,' Chase reminds her, 'and the people involved are undoubtedly in the best interests of Norwich City Football Club.'

There is some debate about how long the financial report into Norwich would take, and whether it is right to expect the club to foot the bill. We also come back to Chase's argument about the danger of his being sued by minority shareholders. 'Mr Chairman,' he is told. 'I can assure you of one thing – and I am sure most people in this room would agree with me – that you would not be sued by a group of minority shareholders. They would be too pleased to see you go.'

This provokes more applause, and another bullet at Chase from someone else: 'I don't think there is a shareholder in this room who doesn't want to see Mr Chase go. He has now given us the opportunity to provide the information to a prospective purchaser whom he has said meets his needs. For heaven's sake, give him the authority and let's get rid of him.'

Chase gets it. He is then picked up on his statement that clubs fall into four categories: (1) the big clubs who, because of their level of support, are financially self-sufficient; (2) those who have a benefactor willing to pour millions into them; (3) those who, because of their low level of support, are dependent on transfer-market income; and (4) those who struggle to make ends meet. 'You have said quite clearly that Norwich fall into category three,' he is reminded. 'I hope that the new board, when they come, see us as category one.'

Chase agrees, but points out: 'Just let me tell you this – two years ago, Touche Ross did a survey of every professional club in the country, and they found that the total profit from the total income was less than £12,000.'

Someone draws his attention to the note in the annual report relating to Norwich's bank loan – £2,116,000 compared to just £116,000 the previous year. 'Can you tell us when the bank loan was taken out and for what reason?'

Chase explains: 'If you look back over the records, you will see that we have usually sold a player for £1 million in the close season.

This time, we bought two players [Rush and Fleck] for that sort of sum. So that in itself is a difference of £2 million, and it has got to be provided from somewhere.'

Chase went on to admit that the drop in income in the Endsleigh League had been greater than he anticipated; and that, 'with the benefit of hindsight', the short-term loans the club had taken out for their stadium facility improvements should have been arranged over a much longer repayment period.

The aggressive woman in the audience sharpened her claws again: 'We seem to be able to find the money to buy things like a carpark, but none to spend on football. Everything about Norwich City is for show. All fur coat and no knickers.'

Laughter and applause – and Chase gets a goal for a change: 'We have no quarrels with you, madam, over the first point.'

'Well, that makes a change.'

Chase reminds the audience of the financial problems other clubs are facing in implementing the all-seater recommendations of the Taylor Report. He concedes that Norwich might not have got the balance right between this and the football side. 'But at least we have most of the expensive work behind us.'

A man challenges him on this. 'So you do actually admit that you have liquidated footballers and turned them into bricks and mortar?'

'We had to bring various sections of the ground up to a standard that was acceptable,' Chase reiterates. 'Lots of clubs haven't done that yet – they still have that expenditure to make.'

His questioner doesn't let go: 'Why are you so negative? Why can't you just be honest and say: "Yes, we did sell footballers to improve the ground"? I am not criticising you for this, I just want you to be truthful. Let me go one stage further; is it not true that you realised that in improving the assets of the club – i.e. bricks and mortar – it would increase the value of your shares?' [Applause.]

Chase denies this. 'Of course, the increase would affect everyone [the shareholders] in the same way.' [Laughter.]

'We are a football club,' a voice protests.

'Yes, I take that point,' Chase says.

'Can you guarantee that no more players will be transferred between now and the start of next season?' he is asked.

'I've learned my lesson,' Chase retorts, referring to the mistake he made over his pledge to keep Chris Sutton. 'Never again will I say "never". All I can say is that we have no offer for any player from any club that we are considering.'

As he is being pressed on this point, Ken Brown comes into the action. He reminds Chase that, though Reading have a comparatively poor stadium, they have recently spent £700,000 in the transfer market to try and lift themselves clear of relegation danger. 'You know as well as I do that if things carry on here as they are, you are going to have the greatest stadium in the world – in the Second Division. That's because you do not understand football.'

When the roar of approval has subsided, someone else asks: 'If the manager came to you and said: "I must have a player before the deadline," what would your answer be?'

'You are asking a hypothetical question.' [Laughter.] 'If he had stumbled on a bargain –'

'But you have sold two bargains [Newsome and Ward], Mr Chase.'

Later, the audience show their amusement again when Chase makes what many would consider a Freudian slip of the tongue. He is asked if manager Gary Megson has the authority to sign players. 'Absolutely – as long as he operates within his budget, he can bring in any loan player that he wishes.'

'Loan?' a voice asks incredulously.

But it is towards the end of this one-and-a-half-hour match of the day that someone gets the most memorable goal. A man says: 'Mr Chase has said on a number of occasions that only a very small minority of the people are against him. Would those in this room who would prefer Mr Chase to go please stand and put their hands up.'

They all did.

On Thursday, 2 May, Roy Blower and thousands of other Norwich fans got the news they had been yearning for: the announcement that Chase had finally called it a day at Carrow Road, and sold his 48,000 shares in the club.

By the start of the season, they had Mike Walker, their managerial idol, back in command of the team – after an 18-month absence from the game – and had resigned themselves to the club having to 'start from scratch' again.

The words were those of Walker, amidst a report that Norwich – said to be £5 million in debt when Chase left – could barely afford to use the state-of-the-art training complex that the old chairman had installed. Walker added: 'I told him [Chase] that if he carried on the way he was going, the club would get relegated and all the hard work would be for nothing. He didn't listen and, in the end, brought the club to its knees. When I think of the team we had, with Chris Sutton, Ruel Fox, Mark Robins, Efan Ekoku, Mark Bowen and the like.

'Now, we are having to try and find those players again from our youth ranks because, heaven knows, we can't buy anyone. The club is quite simply starting again.'

As for Chase, he 'returned to the anonymity of being a Yarmouth builder', as one close Norwich City FC observer put it. It is understood that he got £1,200,000 for his shares, which, if the estimates on what he paid for them were correct, would have given him a profit of between £500,000 and £750,000. That is small beer compared to what he might have got had Norwich still been in the Premiership and healthy enough to have been floated on the Stock Exchange.

Still, he must have been relieved to be out of the firing-line, as indeed Peter Swales was when he left Manchester City in similarly acrimonious circumstances.

'I get a wonderful reception at the other clubs I go to these days,' he had told me. 'Don't get me wrong, I love Manchester City, and I felt I was the luckiest person in the world to have the position I had there. But the nice thing about life now is that I get on better with my children than I have ever done, because previously City came first and foremost in everything I did.'

By the saddest of ironies, the day of Chase's departure was also the day on which Swales died of a heart attack, at the age of 62.

SEVEN

The Balancing Act

Those who felt that the basic principles to which Robert Chase adhered were correct – and, in truth, that applies to most of the chairmen and club owners of today's Premiership and top-of-the-range Football League clubs – the achievement of Ron Noades's Crystal Palace in the 1995–96 season would have been encouraging. It would have emphasised for them that football, being the illogical, unpredictable game it often is, even chairmen who are perceived to have placed a barrier in front of their team's chances of success can easily emerge from the mire smelling of roses. It also emphasised that chairmen, like managers and players, are judged on results, no matter how these results are achieved, and that no single method of achieving results can be conclusively proved to be the best or most desirable.

The fact that Crystal Palace reached the First Division promotion play-off final might not seem particularly significant in itself. After all, Palace are known as one of the yo-yo clubs of English football, having been relegated three times and promoted twice since Noades took over in 1981; as it was only in May 1995 that they last lost their place in the top flight, it was perhaps to be expected that their recent experience there would stand them in good stead at the lower level. But, of course, Palace's success – in this instance, the narrowness with which they missed their promotion target – was rendered remarkable through the high number of star players they sold before the start of the season and by the fact that only £5 million of the £13 million Palace received for those players (among them Gareth Southgate, Richard Shaw, John Salako, Chris Coleman and Chris Armstrong) was spent on replacements.

When I saw Noades, in the 1995 close season, he explained that the financial gap between the Premiership and the First Division was growing wider each season, and that Football League clubs, faced with a loss of revenue then estimated at £3 million, were taking a bigger gamble than ever in not economising. Though he accepted that there was still some financial comfort for them, in the form of their continuing to get a share of the BSkyB television money for one season, he pointed out that the payments were spread over two years. 'On the last occasion we were relegated from the Premiership [in 1993], we had to reduce our bank borrowing limit by £2.5 million, which we did with the money we got from the transfers of Geoff Thomas and Eddie McGoldrick, and the sell-on fee we received from Stan Collymore's move from Southend to Nottingham Forest. This time, we have had to reduce it by £3.5 million.'

He predicted that the First Division would soon represent a 'disaster zone'; that the deficit for relegated clubs would be increased to a 'horrendous' extent by the new improved BSkyB Premiership deal – yet to be agreed at that time – and the limited scope for clubs to make it up with transfer-market sales following the Bosman ruling.

This gloomy picture of the immediate future proved to have much validity when those staggering new TV income figures for the Premiership clubs were announced. In an article in the *Daily Telegraph*, Charlton's manager, Alan Curbishley, echoed Noades' fears when he said: 'In the last three years, the Premier League have pulled further away from the Football League. The latest TV deal with Sky merely underlined that if you are not in the Premiership, you are nowhere. Should West Ham, who are just a few miles from

Charlton, stay in the Premiership for three years and we remain in the First Division, they will receive £24 million in TV sponsorship while our payment will be £3 million. Meanwhile, the Bosman ruling, which dictates that European Union players at the end of their contracts can move for nothing, has already taken effect. I fear that rule being extended to internal transfers. Where will the incentive be for smaller clubs to have youth schemes if, after three years of nurturing a young talent, the player leaves on a free transfer? I simply cannot see clubs bothering.'

So, in some ways, Noades felt that Palace had struck it lucky in having so many saleable players when they did. He also rejected the view that he sold far more than was necessary. He had to look at the whole picture, he argued; a picture in which expenditure relating to stadium developments and, indeed, anything outside football that could give Palace a stronger financial base, were just as important as money being spent on the first team, if not more so. 'You have got to believe what you are doing is right,' he said. 'I've been criticised because some people think we should have bought a player instead of building [Palace's new stand]. I tried to tell them that money provided by the Football Trust is not available for buying a player, nor do you get bank funding over ten years to do so. I try to tell them that the development of our stadium and facilities will eventually help us keep our best players here for all their best years. I want Palace to be one of the big clubs, and the only way we can ever achieve that is to have a stadium that will produce the right income.

'This club's been fair with the players, paid bloody good wages. For example, I have just been after a Premier League centre-half who wants £69,000 a year. Last year, I had players here – and I have just let go of one – on £300,000 a year. But the established big clubs can pay more than that, and when I talk about the need for us to get income that will help us keep these players, I am not talking about gate receipts. Having an average gate of 30,000 or 40,000 is not going to enable us to resist offers for players who can earn maybe double elsewhere. We will get 30,000 or 40,000 because these players are here but the reason for their being here will be our commercial income off the field. There are 5,000 seats in the new stand, for example, and they are all within easy reach of a lounge bar and restaurant facilities. So, on top of the money people have paid to get in, they are also spending £10 while they're here.'

This money, Noades argues, is even more important than the cash that clubs are getting from TV. 'What happens if the BSkyB money disappears tomorrow? What happens if Murdoch suddenly decides that there is no one else in the market and that, instead of raising the price for televising matches, he can afford to push it down? The clubs [who rely on that money to buy the best players] will be in an absolute panic, won't they? It will be as though they have been relegated; they will all be trying to get their £6,000-a-week players off the wage bill. They might think that they will be able to sell a player, but I've heard that before. You can't always sell a player, and there are times when you haven't got one good enough to sell for big money anyway.'

He also pointed out that most of the players Palace sold had themselves demanded transfers, on the basis of improving themselves financially or professionally, or both. They were determined to get away, to put it mildly. Noades recalled: 'Our relegation meant one player's salary dropping from more than £100,000 a year to around £70,000. I said to him: "Look, you did a good job for us last year, so if you give me a list of clubs you would like to go to, and don't ask to go on the transfer list, I will give you a new contract to ensure you don't lose any money by staying here and keep you informed of any enquiries for you." But ten days after giving me the list, he actually put in a transfer request.' Noades added that the player was surprised that he still got his new contract. 'I have prided myself on never breaking my word and I had already promised him that he would not suffer because of our relegation,' Noades explained. As for his decision not to force some of his key players to stay, he says: 'No matter how much ability a player has, it is counter-productive to try and hold on to him if he doesn't want to play for you. What's worse:

having unhappy players, or players of lesser ability who want to play for you?'

For much of the season, most Palace followers would have readily chosen the first alternative. Willing they might have been, but Palace's new team, under a new management structure which had seen Steve Coppell returning to the club in a broad role as their 'technical director', and Ray Lewington and Peter Nicholas working under him as the first- and second-team coaches, seemed a good bet to land up in the Second Division. In February, however, Noades pulled off his masterstroke by appointing David Bassett as team manager. Palace, 16th in the table then, rose to third with a run of only four defeats in 22 matches.

In trying to make some sense of this transformation, you are immediately reminded of what Robert Chase said concerning the importance of the 'chemistry' – the psychological and emotional blend – within a club. He was referring to the chemistry among the team, but in the case of Palace there can be little doubt that it was well nigh perfect between the chairman and the manager. Bassett, seven years younger than Noades, has made his name as something of an artisan professional; as a player he never progressed beyond the unglamorous working-class Football League levels, and as a manager he has seemed fated always to be in charge of teams with limited technical ability. As he once said: 'If a club have money to spend, they go out and get a manager like Kenny Dalglish or Ron Atkinson. If they don't, they call for me. They think: "We're in the shit, Harry will dig us out of it."'

That is very much Noades's type of language – in many ways, his background in the game has been just as unpretentious as Bassett's has been. One clue to his philosophy is that in his choice of Palace staff he has plumped mainly for men with whom he was associated in his non-league days; figures who were happy to devote themselves to the game, away from the public spotlight, without getting anything like the financial rewards and media recognition that their dedication deserved. To be a kindred spirit of Noades, you have to be a 'soccer nut' (his description of himself). 'There are an awful lot of people who are in football because they love it, and who are happy to do it for nothing.' In that category is Jeff Taylor, who was Bassett's assistant at Sheffield United. Noades recalled that he paid Taylor £20 a week to be his manager at Southall in the Isthmian League. 'But he never took it – he gave it to the players. He used to coach the kids at QPR in the evening for no money at all.'

As for Bassett, he and Noades have known each other for more than 30 years, since Bassett, who had gone to the same school in Harrow as Noades's younger brother, played for the Old Boys XI that the then 20-year-old Noades ran. When Bassett was combining his playing career – in amateur and non-league football – with an insurance business, Noades, by then a property developer, rented him an office block he owned in Stanmore. It was on Bassett's advice that Noades, on becoming Southall's chairman, appointed Taylor as his manager at Southall. Bassett played a big part, too, in Noades's decision to buy Wimbledon in 1976. They were in the Southern League in those days and Bassett was one of their key players. Noades recalls; 'Every Monday morning, Dave would come in and talk about the way Wimbledon were being run, the financial problems. So, on his encouragement, I went to see the owner, and bought the club.'

Wimbledon were in the Fourth Division of the Football League when Noades left them for Palace. But he was in charge of both clubs for three weeks, and during this period he switched Wimbledon's manager, Dario Gradi, to Palace, and promoted Bassett, Gradi's Wimbledon assistant, into his position – a decision that launched one of the most remarkable success stories in British football history.

Bassett's arrival at Palace in 1996 was not the first time he had formed a partnership with Noades there; the previous one lasted only a couple of days, when Bassett, appointed Palace's manager on the strength of his steering Wimbledon into the Second Division, did a sudden U-turn back to Plough Lane. 'I suddenly realised Wimbledon were far too good a team to leave behind,' Bassett said.

While Bassett has seen virtually all there is to see at the sharp end of professional football, the same could be said of Noades. Indeed, if there was a training school for league chairmen, he would be its principal tutor. No chairman has served a more thorough apprenticeship than he has; in addition to the Isthmian and Southern Leagues, and the Premiership – how's that for extremes? – he has also held the position in all four divisions of the old Football League.

In working his way up from the very bottom, Noades, intense to the point of appearing almost miserable, has not been a particularly popular figure. He can easily come across as being too opinionated and dogmatic and there are certainly no airs or graces about him. One occasion that his bluntness rebounded against him was in 1991 when he created a major row for making racist remarks in a television documentary on black footballers. Noades was an obvious person to be asked to contribute to the programme, given that his Palace team had a high number of black players. Imagine the reaction he got, therefore, when he said: 'When you're getting into midwinter in England, you need the hard white man to push the artistic black players through.' An unforgivable comment, perhaps, but the sentiments behind it are hardly unheard of in the prejudiced, macho world of English football, especially among the professionals on the shop floor. As far as Noades is concerned, despite his position as a chairman, it is on the shop floor that he truly sees himself. The people there talk his language and he talks theirs.

The most interesting aspect of Noades, however, is that anybody can do what he has done in the game – provided, of course, that they are 'soccer nuts'. 'I just wanted to be involved in football all my life,' he says. 'That's all I ever wanted. I never did any work at school really. When I had to pass the school tech exam at 13, to get a scholarship to the polytechnic to study accountancy and commerce, I did. But, other than that, I was only really interested in football.'

Born and raised in Kilburn, north-west London, Noades's adult playing experience, as an outside-right, was restricted to his school Old Boys team. He had to stop playing at 30 because of a lung condition, so his enormous enthusiasm for the game was channelled into coaching and refereeing. As a football-watcher, he had been particularly keen on Derby County, one of the most successful teams in the First Division when he was a boy. Once he had begun to establish himself in the property business, following a number of selling and marketing jobs, he and his brother Colin (now a fellow Palace director) bought Derby season-tickets. A block of flats Noades built was named Derby House, and one sub-development even bore the names of Derby players.

But it is his development of football clubs that has stimulated Noades the most. No football debate on the subject of how clubs can fully exploit their potential – at least in the financial sense – would be truly authoritative without an input from him, for the simple reason that he has faced the challenge at a level at which this sort of expertise has been most needed. The principle of clubs standing on their own two feet, of helping themselves rather than waiting for hand-outs from others, was first instilled into Noades at Southall. Under his command, the club, which had just been relegated and which, he says, was literally handed to him, were promoted the following season, and managed to consolidate their position. More pertinent to Noades was their progress off the field. He recalls: 'You paid all your wages then through the bars, and one of the first things I did was to rebuild the clubhouse to create more [bars]. Because of that, we were able to raise the weekly salary of the players from £48 to £208.' He was constantly improving other ground amenities, too – but, as the stadium was owned by the local council, he inevitably began to question the logic behind this commitment. It was then that Bassett persuaded him to take a step up the chairman ladder at Wimbledon.

It wasn't the first time that Wimbledon, owned by a man called Bernie Coleman, had been in financial difficulty. On the previous occasion they had been fortunate enough to get a lifeline by drawing Don Revie's Leeds United giants in the FA Cup – a £35,000 gate. Twelve months later, though, they were in trouble again, which is where Noades came in. 'You can only buy a club when the directors have had enough or can't handle it,' he points out. 'When a club are buoyant, you never get in.' Still, to him, nothing can compare with the excitement of putting an ailing club on its feet, especially a club where survival itself is an achievement.

He bought around 70 per cent of the Wimbledon shares from Bernie Coleman for just £2,768, a deal which included the freehold of the ground ('But there was a restriction on the freehold that meant it was never worth more than £8,000,' Noades said) and the pub alongside it. 'Bernie could have sold the club for £15,000 to Jim Gregory [then QPR's chairman] but he was worried that it would become just a nursery for QPR. I guaranteed him that Wimbledon would carry on, but I couldn't see how it would be financially viable without the pub. He had a 21-year lease on it, and he just gave it to me. So the club ended up with a pub, and I was able to make it work.

'What I did was to put together a group of people who all had something to contribute – I mean, if you were an electrician, and you were prepared to do all the electrical work at the club, you could be on the board. That's the way it worked. I put together what I would call a working committee and we more or less did a lot of the building work ourselves.'

In his first season, Wimbledon won the Southern League Championship for the third successive year and, thanks to his canvassing zeal, were elected to the Football League. Noades recalled the pride he experienced when he told the media that Wimbledon did not have an average gate break-even target. 'They said: "What do you mean?" I said: "Because of the way we have built up our commercial income off the pitch, with the pub, the bars and everything else, we can pay our way without attracting that many spectators."'

Indeed, this has remained a notable characteristic of Wimbledon FC, who make their money from selling players and whose support is so limited and problematic that their budgets are based on the premise of not getting any spectators at all. Hence their dream of moving out of the financial straightjacket imposed on them by their location – and by no longer having a ground of their own – by basing themselves in the English-football-crazy city of Dublin.

Noades himself saw the writing on the wall for Wimbledon some time ago – in 1981, in fact, when he led a consortium into the purchase of Crystal Palace. He wanted to have both clubs under his belt, but once the FA stamped on that idea, Noades was more than happy to switch to Selhurst Park. He explained: 'One of the reasons was the pre-emption clause on the ground, which meant that if Wimbledon ever got into financial difficulty, or went into liquidation, they would have to sell the ground back to the local authority for £8,000 [the price they had originally paid for it]. So I was locked into a situation similar to the one at Southall, where I was personally having to find the funds or underwrite the loans for ground improvements without having the ability to secure it on the freehold. We wanted to extend the roof of the stand behind the goal to provide cover for 1,500 more people, but it was going to cost £600,000. Then, suddenly, the Palace shares [76 per cent] became available at £600,000 [from the chairman, Ray Bloye], and I thought: "This is ridiculous – we can buy Palace for that money and play there."'

Crystal Palace, nosediving towards the Second Division, were £1.5 million in debt and gates had dropped from 30,000 to 10,000 in two years. Initially, he says, the eight-man consortium which bought 76 per cent of the Palace shares was intended to include himself, Coleman and his friend Sam Hammam. But Hammam, who had become a major shareholder in Wimbledon four years earlier, changed his mind and elected instead to buy the Wimbledon stock of Noades and Coleman for £40,000.

Hammam – best man at Noades's second marriage, and godfather to his children – struck it lucky when that pre-emption clause on Plough Lane was removed. Moreover, Wimbledon, unlike Palace, are still in the Premiership.

But if Noades has learned anything at Selhurst Park, it is patience. 'The biggest mistake I made when I came to Palace was that I was conceited enough to think I could change everything in 12 months – just wave a magic wand and everything would be fine. The debts were enormous; I found more bills every day. I remember our architect, who had been with me at Wimbledon, walking in and asking: "What do you want me to do with my accounts?" I said: "What do you mean?" He said: "The invoices I haven't put in. I thought I was doing you a favour – I haven't invoiced you for anything for five years."'

To Noades, it can take time for the right foundations to be laid at a club and he's happy that the base on which he is building Palace will be strong enough to enable them to bypass most of their rivals. Certainly, assuming that Hammam never does get that move to Dublin, or anywhere else where the demand for Premiership football is not being satisfied, Noades has no doubts that his move will turn out to be a wise one. 'I wanted to run a successful football club – that's all I have ever really wanted to do – and the prime requisite for that is that you have to have a big catchment area. Wimbledon never had one at Plough Lane – look at a map and you'll see that one side of the ground is Richmond Park – there are no houses. Now I look at our catchment area and I think it is as good as that of any club in the league.

'I think Wimbledon are a great club, and Sam has done brilliantly. But Sam wants to be in charge of a big club, and he is frustrated in my view because he knows that Wimbledon will never get the support to enable them to get into that category. I think Sam would like to buy Palace if he could.

'Wimbledon would have unbelievable financial problems if they were relegated. That's what I mean when I talk about the need to make sure you are not financially vulnerable. If I knew that relegation would mean financial disaster for us, I couldn't sleep at night.'

His determination to lay solid foundations brings us back to Palace's failure to return to the Premiership at their first attempt. As he said before the start of the 1995–96 season: 'Contrary to what a lot of people might think, it is going to be easier to get out of the First Division this season, but it's also going to be easier for teams to come straight back down. The market now is such that if you were to go up this season with, say, seven players good enough to play in the Premiership, the four that aren't are going to cost you £3.5 million each to replace: that is £14 million. You can't do it. So you've got to build a team that will get you into the Premiership and which will not need much money spent on it.'

This is less of a problem to some chairmen and club owners than it is to others. There are still men in English football for whom money is no object in their pursuit of excellence on the field. Think of Sir John Hall at Newcastle United, and the passion – and financial boldness – which has been poured into the dream of emulating Manchester United.

EIGHT

The Way Ahead?

Rick Parry, the Premiership's chief executive, inevitably chose his words carefully when attempting to paint a general picture of the top clubs' chairmen – effectively his employers – as a group. 'You have to recognise – and I don't mean this in a derogatory way – that placing powerful entrepreneurs into a regulatory, democratic framework does present interesting tensions.'

Parry stressed that the men who run the Premiership clubs now pull together for the good of the game much more cohesively than they did in the early days of the League, when the residual suspicion of each other's motives – emanating from the determination of giants like Manchester United and Arsenal to cut off increasingly bigger slices of the overall financial cake when they were part of the old Football League – made Parry's job a diplomacy nightmare. Not surprisingly, on the grounds of political correctness, he is reticent about going into details of the highly charged atmosphere behind the scenes, the petty feuds and squabbles, that made the Premiership chairmen's meetings potentially explosive. But one prominent source says: 'If you can imagine it as a boxing bill, then the main bouts were David Dein against Ken Bates and Ron Noades – and Sam Hammam against everybody.'

As Wimbledon have long been the club at the bottom end of the Premiership in financial terms, Hammam has been more sensitive than anyone about the prospect of the comparative minnows of the game being swallowed up by the big fish. On the basis that nothing bonds a football team together more tightly than a sense of injustice, Hammam, far from attempting to get rid of Wimbledon's under-class football image – the perception of the team as an undisciplined rabble – has cleverly exploited it.

Wimbledon are at their most effective when they feel that the world is against them; and, at times when they might have felt that they were becoming more popular, it has not been unusual for Hammam to take it upon himself to try and dissuade them from such thoughts. For a match at West Ham, for example, he daubed the dressing-room walls with graffiti alluding to the most unpopular aspects of his team's approach to the game. He was also an early visitor to their dressing-room before a match at Blackburn, to soak their playing kit in cold water.

As Manchester United manager Alex Ferguson has said: 'Nothing motivates players more than anger.'

The same could be said of chairmen like Hammam, as United's Martin Edwards has found. United, of course, are at the other end of the financial scale to Wimbledon, and as this has been reflected by their stance in discussions over Premiership policy, the relationship between Edwards and Hammam has not been without some friction. 'At one of the early Premiership meetings,' one insider recalls, 'Sam was so upset by something Martin said that he was virtually chasing him round the table. No blows were struck, but the confrontation was quite heated, to say the least.'

At another meeting, when Hammam was arguing for a bigger centralised pot of Premiership money – basically, the rich doing a bit more to help the poor – Dein retorted: 'Sam, do us a favour – get your hands out of our pockets.'

'In his football dealings, Sam is the epitome of the Middle Eastern market trader,' says PFA chief executive Gordon Taylor, one of Hammam's biggest admirers. 'He's unbelievable, really – I mean, he has you almost crying at transfer tribunals. His big line is: "Oh, we are so poor; we can't manage and all the big clubs are against us." Dealing with Sam is a bit like going into a bazaar and not being able to get past the market trader unless you buy something from him to help feed his starving family.' Taylor recalled he and his wife being guests of Hammam at a Wimbledon v Manchester United match. 'All through the game, he is talking to my wife and bending her ear about the unfair publicity his players get, telling her that they are like his sons and why is it that everybody keeps having a go at them . . .' Taylor shook his head. 'Unbelievable.'

A number of his Wimbledon players would readily endorse the view. Take striker Dean Holdsworth, whose wagers with Hammam over the player's goal totals for the club each season have included the Hammam offer of a Ferrari – and even a camel. The latter was said to have been offered to Holdsworth in the event of his scoring 15 goals in the 1994–95 season – a target which the player was no doubt grateful to miss. It made a change. 'I can't degrade him any more that I have already,' Holdsworth was quoted as saying. 'He had to kiss my backside in front of the team after I reached my target last season, and the season before that, he had to spend £7,000 to have a bronze statue made of me.'

Despite such leanings towards eccentricity and unorthodoxy, Hammam's philosophy concerning Wimbledon – and all clubs like them – does raise some disturbing thoughts about the path which English football at the top level is being taken down. During the 1995–96 season, when those clubs were perceived as having taken another step towards a full-scale European Super League through the decision to extend the league format of the Champions Cup, Hammam made the most impassioned of speeches – in *The Sun*:

> Do not believe what was said in Geneva [when European Super League talks involving Manchester United, Liverpool and Arsenal ended with no signs of their getting beyond the preliminary discussion stage]. This [the change in the Champions Cup League competition] is the first step towards a

Super League. It is inevitable and is what the big clubs in this country want. Eventually, the élite in England will be playing AC Milan. The so-called big boys left behind will make up the Premiership, and the rest of us will turn off the lights and go home. Just imagine the situation in Geneva. There, they [the big clubs] are talking about the future, what they can do for themselves. I wonder if anybody said: 'What about Wimbledon and Crewe?' Manchester United do not want to play Wimbledon. They want to play Real Madrid, Barcelona or AC Milan. It will not be long before we stop calling clubs like that English clubs. They will be European clubs, and the bigger they get, the smaller we become. There are hundreds of Wimbledons – do we really want those clubs to disappear? The game has become obsessed with money and power. We deserve more from the game. I will not let those clubs leave us behind – why should so many clubs throw away tradition, everything they have stood for, just because a few clubs want to get richer and richer playing in Europe?

Whatever the merits of that argument, Hammam deserved full marks for making it so forcibly, at the expense of being labelled a hypocrite. His tale of woe, and that of other Premiership czars in a similar position, was precisely the same as the one the clubs in the old Football League expounded when the likes of Wimbledon threw their hats into the Premiership ring and helped turn the élite group's dream of a First Division breakaway into reality. It was inevitable that even at this level there would be a growing gap between the haves and the have-nots, that the rich would get richer and the poor poorer. It was inevitable if only because of the mentalities of the men running the top-of-the range clubs – men like Sir John Hall, whose transformation of Newcastle, in tandem with a similarly dynamic, singleminded team manager in Kevin Keegan, has in many ways been as remarkable as the one which Jack Walker initiated at Blackburn.

In understanding why the presence of men such as Hall – or rather what they stand for – has provoked almost as much fear in the game as respect and admiration, it is tempting to draw political analogies. In common with other members of the new breed of chairman, Hall was helped towards his personal fortune by the environment created by Margaret Thatcher's policies. Politically, the position he has taken up on the right wing now seems as extreme as the one he once filled on the left. It is only to be expected, therefore, that those policies (or rather the personal enterprise, capitalistic philosophies behind them) should be mirrored in his approach to football.

Hall is a miner's son who was born and raised in a terraced house near Ashington, County Durham. He spent the first seven years of his working life down the pit, the last five as a mining surveyor. Today, he is a millionaire many times over and lives in the 5,000-acre baronial estate of Northumberland's Wynward Park, in a 70-room nobleman's palace – Wynward Hall – in which the chandeliers alone cost him £100,000 to restore. He bought the whole shooting match from the Marquis of Londonderry in 1987. It is not known what he paid for it, but suffice it to say that the Marquis openly admitted that he could no longer afford to run it and Hall has spent a total of £3 million bringing it up to standard.

He once described himself as 'a Conservative with a social conscience', which has been borne out by the knighthood he received for his part in the regeneration of the north-east. In an interview in *The Independent*, he said: 'I was born into the Labour Party, and my father took me to hear its great speakers, Bevin, Bevan and Attlee. I owe everything in my life to the Labour government of 1945. They said to us: "Go out, educate yourselves, be better than your fathers." But the trouble with the Labour Party was that they never kept up with the aspirations of the people they'd created. They gave my father dignity and me a grammar-school education; but my father died on £12 a week and my mother had £1 a week pension. I said to myself: "Is that what it's all been for?" I started questioning the system. You may not agree but she [Margaret Thatcher] changed the face of UK plc. She tried to liberate everybody, but the press and the intellectuals couldn't understand her.'

Having bought into a small estate agency, Hall was 36 when he started to liberate himself. It led to the formation of a property development company, Cameron Hall Developments, and the hitting of a massive financial jackpot when he took the gamble of raising £200 million to build Europe's biggest shopping mall, the now famous Metro Centre in Gateshead.

Hall, whose other public claim to fame – apart from Newcastle United FC – is that he is chairman of the National Lottery Millennium Committee and is a man who thinks big in everything he does. Occasionally, you get the impression that he can be too bold for his own good, a feeling that takes on particular significance in the context of his Newcastle role when you consider that Keegan is similarly headstrong and impulsive by nature and that the Newcastle team have yet to reveal the solid consistency of which champions are made.

Keegan's appointment as manager was made by the board rather than by Hall, whose position as chairman then was belied by his not having a controlling interest in the club and who had pledged his support of Keegan's predecessor, Ossie Ardiles. Keegan briefly walked out on Newcastle 38 days later, when he did not get the money for new players that he claims he was promised. But since then, he and Hall – both bursting with energy and restless ambition – have revealed themselves as kindred spirits. 'Now, it's brilliant,' Keegan has said. 'If I want a player, I can sign that player today, not tomorrow, or next week or after a board meeting.'

Unfortunately, the negative aspect of their breathless approach was illustrated by the manner in which Newcastle cut their own throats in the 1995–96 Championship race, after being 12 points ahead. Those acquainted with the ultra-thrustful personalities of Hall and Keegan might well have deemed it typical that Newcastle should ultimately blow up through an overemphasis on attack, not to mention the gamble of buying Faustino Asprilla and trying to accommodate such an unpredictable individualist in their team instead of keeping faith with the personnel and system of play that had stood them in good stead earlier. Still, Hall was not too disappointed, arguing that a Newcastle Championship triumph in 1996 would have been ahead of the development schedule he had originally laid down when taking over the club.

One crucial part of that development schedule lies in Newcastle's plans to become a PLC, an aim which had rendered the price they paid Alan Shearer far less of a gamble than it might have seemed in view of the player's exceptionally high international profile and his ability to boost the club's income off the field. Whether Shearer and any of the other big-name players at Newcastle can give them the success expected on the field remains to be seen. By the start of the 1996–97 season, the gap between Newcastle and Manchester United seemed as big as ever. Particularly worrying for Newcastle was that even their supremacy in the North-east was being threatened – notably by Middlesbrough, a club who themselves have undergone a remarkable transformation under the chairmanship of Steve Gibson and management of Keegan's ex-England team-mate, Bryan Robson, and whose line-up includes such glittering individualists as former Juventus striker Fabrizio Ravanelli, the Brazilian pair Juninho and Emerson, and Nick Barmby.

For the time being, however, most chairmen's eyes are on Hall. His plans for Newcastle, combined with his in-built distaste of being in a position where he is not in charge of his own destiny, bring us back to what Rick Parry was saying about those Premiership hierarchy 'tensions'.

Certainly, when listening to Hall on the subject of Newcastle's progress since he became chairman in February 1992 – when they were £6.5 million in the red and near the bottom of the old Second Division – and his plans for their future, you can readily appreciate why the likes of Wimbledon are so neurotic about theirs.

In an interview in the *Irish Times* in March 1996, Hall stressed that the money he had poured into the club to help put them back on their feet – initially £5 million – was an investment, not a gift, and said: 'We are paying for the sins of our fathers and the lack of money being put into football clubs over the years, but we do treat anything we put in now as an investment. We [his son Douglas and associate Freddie Sheppard] expect a return on that investment because anyone who comes in from the private sector and just treats football as a whim will find that football seriously damages your wealth.

'So far, it has been our job to get the base in place, and now we've built that [a 36,000 all-seater stadium in which all but 6,000 places are filled by season-ticket holders]. We needed a team that people would want to watch, which is there now [at a transfer market cost of more than £30 million]. When we took over, the club's turnover was £4.5 million; this year it will be £40 million, and the target is somewhere around £65 million or £75 million. At that stage, it has to start paying its way.'

Hall, not content with having a successful football club, has set his sights on Newcastle United being part of a vast sport and re-creational empire similar to those in which some of the soccer giants in other countries – notably Real Madrid and Barcelona – have become integrated. He has already taken control of Gosforth Rugby Club, a process which has led to the signing of Rob Andrew as manager, and a number of international players, and has also brought his vision of sporting excellence to bear on a local athletics club and the city's leading ice-hockey team. There is also the question of 320 acres of land he has bought, with the aim of turning it into an academy from which the future generations of British sporting champions will spring.

'We have a lot of plans for the next few years. We're going to make money out of everything that is humanly possible to allow us to compete with the best sides in Europe. We want to set up a television station [Magpie TV] when the city is fully cabled, which should be within two years, and we want to establish the Newcastle Sporting Club, which will bring in families interested in all sorts of different sports. We're aiming for 100,000 members, and when we have them, I'll sell them insurance through the club, and holidays through the club . . . the possibilities are endless.'

You can get dizzy just listening to him, and as one observer says: 'For all his undoubted drive, wisdom and vision, Hall can occasionally irritate some of his fellow chairmen. His strong personality can make him appear to be lecturing them, talking to them like schoolkids. They all have big egos, and the one thing they don't like is being seen to be led by someone else.'

The big question, though, is whether they are heading in a direction that is good for British football. Gordon Taylor believes that they are – up to a point. One of the things Taylor most likes about the new breed is that he feels they are more understanding of the players' problems than their predecessors were. 'A number of them are almost contemporaries of the players and can relate to them.' Taylor, conscious of the need to keep as many professional clubs in business as possible, is concerned about the inflationary wages being paid to players nowadays. 'The chairmen have been doing our job for us,' he quips. 'In some ways, their determination to be successful has probably been a bigger factor in the escalation of players' wages at the top level than the PFA have been. People describe top players as being mercenary but, if that really is the case, I think that chairmen have encouraged them to be that way because that's the way they are themselves – to an extent that's how they have made their money in their own businesses.' Mindful of the Thatcherite principles to which men like Hall adhere, he is also sensitive about the way in which they view his trade union's influence on the game. He is no Arthur Scargill but he admits: 'I've had fall-outs with all of them.'

Some are more powerful than others. Perhaps the most high-profile chairman in the world is AC Milan's Silvio Berlusconi, until recently Italy's Prime Minister. He was the man who set the ball rolling for a full-scale European Super League some years ago, and who could be described as the catalyst for the changes to the format of the European Champions Cup competition. For years the competition was the *de luxe* version of the FA Cup. But the drawback in this for the owners of the European giants was the possibility of their being knocked out in an early round, and thus missing out on the income from TV, advertising and sponsorship deals. For men like Berlusconi, the results of the football clubs they owned were too closely linked to the success of their business empires as a whole for them to be put at risk by the vagaries of the game. Moreover, in order to truly exploit their commercial potential, they deemed it necessary to have as many European ties as possible against clubs of a similar stature.

That has left us with a situation in which the number of teams in the competition has been reduced from more than 40 to 24 (all from the top-ranked nations), with eight going straight into four league groups and the other 16 enduring play-offs for the right to join them. One of the advantages for the 16 group teams is that they are guaranteed three home matches.

So one can appreciate why Hammam argues that a full-scale European Super League is around the corner, and that the first casualty of that could be the domestic leagues. There is also the alternative threat of Berlusconi and the other European football big-shots setting up a world franchise league of their own.

Exciting times ahead? Well, that's one way of looking at it. The Arsenal chairman who fell off his chair would not doubt see it differently.